MAKING A MICROBUSINESS

MAKING A *Micro* BUSINESS

The Bootstrapper's Checklist of 78 Action Items for your Startup

ANGELA FORD

TAG
BOOKS

Published in the United States by TAG Books,
a division of TAG Properties, Inc., Chicago, IL
www.thisistag.com

TAG Books and colophon are registered
trademarks of TAG Properties, Inc.

TAG Books books are available at special discounts for bulk purchases, for sales
promotions or corporate use. Special editions, including personalized covers,
excerpts of existing books, or books with corporate logos, can be created in large
quantities for special needs. For more information, contact Premium Sales at (312)
447-0400 or e-mail specialmarkets@thisistag.com

ISBN 978-0-9965007-0-8

Library of Congress Cataloging-in-Publication Data

Ford, Angela
Making a microbusiness The Bootstrapper's Checklist of
78 Action Items for your Startup / by Angela Ford.

　　　p.　cm.
Includes Index.

1. New business enterprises – Management 2. Entrepreneurship I. Title
II. Title: Making A Microbusiness

ISBN:　978-0-9965007-0-8
eISBN:　978-0-9965007-1-5

Printed in the United States of America

Book Design:　Angela Ford
Illustrations:　Paolo Lopez DeLeon

10　9

First Edition

To Steven, who always believed in
all of my microbusinesses
without question or doubt.

TABLE OF CONTENTS

INTRODUCTION

INTRODUCTION

For 25 of my 50+ years of life, I have been self-employed full-time. From many books I have read, the next sentence would mention the millions of dollars I made and the world leaders I have encountered. But that's not me. I made an honest living. That's it. I bought some buildings. I have traveled to different countries. I got married. I got divorced. I have one son. American-dream stuff. I have a wonderful life.

It took me a long time to realize how fortunate I was to be self-employed. The day-to-day hustles, the thrill of a sale, the agony of failure and rejection had the same payoff as any great sport. My life was an ebb and flow of money. I lived a feast and famine existence. But what I did not have was an alarm clock. I did not have "the Sword of Damocles" hanging over my head. "What will my review say?" "Will she give me the promotion?" "Does he think I should be fired?" The questions often thought about right before the Monday morning heart attack.

Instead, my future is mine to shape and mold. Most of my friends are entrepreneurs because we have the time and flexibility to meet and build those relationships. Not only do we run microbusinesses, we collaborate for charity events to improve our communities and we plan fun parties, strictly for celebrations. Instead of working myself to death for the arbitrary measure of millions of dollars, I live a great life right now.

I graduated college in the 1980s. Back then the formula was simple. Get a Bachelor's Degree in something and then sort out your job offers. Buy a house. Get a car, stay on the job 40 years and then draw your pension. All of my peers and I defined success by our starting salary at the corporation and the type of car we bought with our first paychecks. Small businesses were for those that could get college degrees that were the permission slips to live in Utopia. We got jobs, we got direct deposit of our paychecks, we came to work on time, we got raises and we bought more things.

Then the world changed completely.   Technological innovation replaced the need for us college folk. A corporation no longer needed ten vice presidents, when two with smartphones would do just fine. The only real skills they had honed were how to get along with people or how to work in specific corporate cultures. I watched my friends get laid off from jobs at "the sausage factory" where they had no idea how the sausages were made.

Their hustling skills don't exist anymore.   They haven't negotiated a deal since their trip to a flea market 20 years ago. Like a high school track star that sat on the couch for 20 years, this reintegration into making money will be difficult. But it's possible.

The younger generations have it easier.   If they've paid attention, they have seen the ups and downs of the elders. They know that at least one alternative revenue stream from a main job is good for the soul.

This book is for the young and the old. It is for people who are seriously about to start their businesses or improve their business and could use valuable action steps to succeed and turn a strong profit.

When I started my first business, I took a ton of entrepreneurial classes. I'm still a little bitter about that lost time and treasure. I didn't learn much about how to build MY business. I learned what other people had done. This book doesn't rehash what Thomas Edison or Steve Jobs did. It is about what you can do, right now with what you have. Grab a pencil. It's your book. Make some notes! Let's get started!

WHAT'S REAL?

The world is changing. People do business with people all around the world. This globalization has allowed savvy businesses to downsize in order to survive. It's like a moving train. You get on or get under.

In a global economy, salaries stabilize. For many, that means salaries shrink. Technology has eliminated the need for many of the jobs that my colleagues once sought for success. Companies that previously needed many vice presidents can now be extremely efficient with a few. Too many of my friends have been laid off from upper management positions to find they haven't developed skills or passions to survive this new world order. The truth is, finding another six-figure-salary job where scheduling meetings and speaking intelligently are the primary requirements, is very hard.

A successful household is now measured by quality of life, not quantity of acquisitions. Building a microbusiness is not just for those who cannot launch the next Fortune 500 business; it's for those who want to be the masters of their own destiny. They live in communities that support neighborhood establishments with unique businesses. Successful people have revenue streams, not just jobs.

The equalizer for the new world is the Internet. A one-man operation can look just as sleek and polished as a 500-employee operation. If the one-man shop can deliver a great product in a timely manner, it can be successful, too.

Whether you've been laid off or are concerned about future employment, you should hone a skill you're passionate about and create a revenue stream around it.

There are many books that showcase successful entrepreneurs, what they have done and how they started. This book is a compilation of actionable steps YOU should take to grow your microbusiness.

START: Make a declaration, I will start/continue this microbusiness.

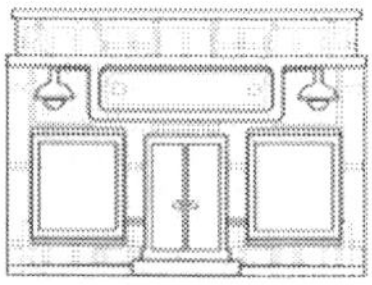

CHAPTER 1

BEGINNINGS

THE HUSTLEMAN MODEL

Right near my home is the train station to downtown. Every business day, there's a guy out there with a plain white truck with all kinds of items for sale. Throw pillows, wash cloths, packaged snacks, coffee in the winter and snow cones in the summer. He has a sandwich board sign on the sidewalk in front of the truck that says: Hustleman. He sells umbrellas when it's raining and skullcaps when the temperature plummets. He is the consummate opportunist. But he is as reliable as the sun. When he's not there, I'm concerned. It's crude, but it's a decent business.

The key to a successful microbusiness is *The Hustleman Model*. You've got this product that people want or need and will pay for it. You are set up in the location where they can easily get it from you. And, you've got to sell it for at least twice what you paid for it.

So back to the Hustleman: He's in the perfect location -- a train stop with a great deal of people going to and from work daily. He keeps a flexible inventory of what his customers need, want and will pay for immediately.

My other favorite hustler is the Water Man. In the city, on a hot summer day, you always find someone selling ice-cold bottles of water to people in cars at major intersections for $1. These people come to these corners with coolers of ice with bottled water. They can purchase a case of 24 bottles of water at a retail outlet for $6 after tax. That is $.25 per bottle. For every bottle sold, the gross profit is $.75! When a sporting event lets out, these men sell hundreds of bottles a day!

Whatever business you open, some component of that business should have a "Hustleman" feature. If you are a restaurant, one of your food items should be the easy profit. If you have a bar, pour soft drinks from the fountain, NOT in bottles or cans. The fountain sodas cost pennies a glass...you're practically printing money. And if you're a vendor with a cart, have the cold water on the hot days.

STEP 1: Have a "Hustleman feature" in your business model. Have something that sells fast that costs you little, but yields a large margin.

A HOBBYIST OR A BUSINESS?

Which do you have?

A hobbyist sells a product or provides a service that they do for fun, sport or side hustle. This isn't how he's going to feed his family. This isn't how he's going to pay the primary bills. His endeavor brings people joy and provides him with extra income.

Someone with a business sells a product or provides a service. The main goal is for the business to provide primary income for the operator with possibly more employees and other means of growth.

Somewhere in the middle between the two is the microbusiness. This hobby vs. business comparison happens on a spectrum rather being a hard and fast contrast. There are no absolutes. The reason you make a determination between the two early is to be honest with yourself. When you set goals for your business, be honest about what you want to achieve. Often times we are taught to believe that going into business means we must aspire to grow a company to a massive scale by hiring a ton of employees and eventually releasing an initial public offering (IPO) for public stock.

Making a microbusiness is not about making a billion dollars right now. It is about creating a quality of life where you can provide for your family, improve your community and enjoy some of life's pleasures. As you create a checklist for your business, you want to set realistic goals. If you're leaning towards hobbyist, it will be fine to aim to make a few hundred dollars per week. If you're creating a microbusiness, you need to plan to make enough to support your life and lifestyle.

Keeping in mind what your business model is, take this brief quiz:

1. I like doing this sometimes, but not all the time. Y   N

2. Even if there were no money, I would do this.   Y   N

3. If I had a million dollars, I would still do this.   Y   N

4. I could do this happily six hours per day.   Y   N

5. I could inspire a few people to help me do this. Y   N

What is the assessment of the quiz? If you answer the first question as yes, you are leaning toward being a hobbyist. If you answered no to 2 through 5, then you should reconsider whether you have picked the right business to enter. To be successful, you have to want to do this and enjoy doing it. If not, you are inviting a lot of stress into your life. You may be better off pursuing a good job. You may not want a true microbusiness, you may just want to make some money. I'm not about that life. I think that paper chasing leads to depression and Monday morning heart attacks. Dare to believe you can start as a hobbyist and move to a microbusiness pursuing a passion-filled life, not just someone trying to make more money.

STEP 2: Honestly determine if your microbusiness is a hobby or a small business endeavor. Either is fine, but take care not to be just a money chaser.

THE NAME OF THE GAME

Let's name the business. Deciding a name for your business will be one of the most important decisions you make. Resist the desire to name the enterprise something strictly personal or exotic. Every time someone says or reads the name of your business, it should help people understand what you are selling.

Retail businesses need to attract drive-by and walk-by customers. The name needs to communicate what you are selling or you will have to spend additional money on marketing. When the name is descriptive, it is not only easier to market on the Web in search engines, but potential customers are more drawn to specific names. Your name should help your business and the logo should provide a visual that drives home the same point.

It may seem like I'm stating the obvious, but think of a retail area in your own neighborhood. Name five businesses in the retail area. I'll give you five of the operating businesses in the neighborhood where I grew up:

1. Walgreens
2. Maxine's
3. Thomas' Restaurant

4. Checkers

5. Popeye's

Three out of five of these are national chains. Walgreens is a household name due to a strong national presence and aggressive advertising. Checkers and Popeye's are national fast food chains with large advertising budgets. Thomas' Restaurant is a local short-order, family-friendly restaurant and Maxine's is a clothing store that caters specifically to mature African-American women. There is a giant awning that says Maxine's. Everyday, hundreds of cars pass by. If for some reason you're stuck at a red light in a very specific spot, you may glance in that direction and see the clothing inside the window. Otherwise, you may never think twice about Maxine's. The generic name is a missed opportunity being that it is not supported by a big budget advertising campaign.

Another potential missed opportunity in a name is the vague business card. If you have a service business, when you hand someone your card, it should be clear what service you are providing. Ideally, you should put this information in the name, but at the very least it ought to be in the job title or the slogan. Here's another example:

Acme Enterprises

Acme Engineering Consultants

Acme Midwest Engineering Consultants

Each name gets more descriptive. When people are looking at new companies, they are more drawn to niche businesses.

Keep in mind that when you make your own name part of the title, you have boxed yourself into a corner.   People will primarily want to deal with you. Everyone else will feel like a poor substitute. If you are going to build your brand around your skillset, then the strategy works.

I'm from Chicago.   Three of my FAVORITE brunch places have some of the best names. It's the main reason I not only found them, but also why I wanted to try them out:

1. Batter & Berries
2. Yolk
3. Brunch

What do you think?   These are very creative names. They communicate that the businesses are food places that serve breakfast or brunch.   Their logos are equally engaging and informative.   Their entrees are as creative and fun as their names.

STEP 3: Create a name for your business that describes your product or services.

WHO EXACTLY IS THE CUSTOMER?

Knowing your customer is the key to a successful microbusiness. Businesses that try to appeal to everyone actually appeal to no one. You want to be able to casually state your customer in one sentence:

"We cater to young urban professionals who grab healthy meals to and from work."

"We focus on athletic women who work out regularly and care about the quality of their workout attire."

"This neighborhood bar services a blue-collar clientele that likes to grab a drink on their way home from work."

"Our product is for seniors already retired but interested in travel."

"My legal practice is 60 percent divorce and 40 percent real estate closings. Both for middle-aged, middle-class residents of my county."

"Ours is a family-friendly diner for locals who want to eat out and have fun."

"This butcher shop provides high quality meats for upwardly-mobile adults concerned about their health and locally-sourced foods."

"My sundries shop exists for business professionals in this building who need quick snacks and magazines as they come and go to work."

"Our dry cleaner store services all residents in a five-mile radius."

Here's what you need to know about your customer:
- Demographics – average age, gender (if gender is relevant);
- Status in life – student, commuter, family, bachelor, retiree
- Lifestyle – athletic, sedentary, pet lover, shopper
- Economics – luxury, middle-class spender, economy shopper, thrift shopper

Once you honestly define your customer, all of your focus will be centered on the customer's interests. Your website, your business card, your tweets and your newsletters will speak to this customer.

Now we're ready for the market survey. Think of 10 people you know that fit your customer description. This is your focus group. Ask them to commit to giving you feedback on your strategy. If you're selling a product, you should have it on hand. Friends and family love to help, especially when you're not asking them for money. When you finish the design of your website, the layout of your store, etc., show these ideas to the group. If you don't have the layout of your microbusiness in renderings, download renderings of the layouts of three or four similar businesses and ask which one is most inviting. It will help you understand your local customer's interpretation of a nice place. Some of your questions should include:

1. What do you think about this product?
2. Is this the price you would be comfortable paying?
3. How often would you buy this product?
4. By the look of this logo, can you tell what we are selling?
5. Does this website look attractive to you?
6. What social media do you use?
7. What else would you like to see us offer?
8. Would you come to this location with this decor?
9. How often do you order products online?
10. Are you more likely to buy this if it's on sale?

If you can get your virtual focus group, or advisory group together at the same time, that would be ideal. They would be inspired by each other's comments and you could have one result. If not, meet with them individually or in small groups. Compile the feedback and make adjustments based on what you are hearing. Your microbusiness should appeal to your customer base.

STEP 4: Clearly identify your customer. Find 10 people who fit your customer base to form your initial focus group.

THE IMPORTANCE OF NICHE

Trying to be everything to everybody is a small business killer. What you want to be is the best to a very specific group of people. Knowing your customers and how best to improve their situation is the way to go.

Can you describe your niche in a sentence?

If you've got a vendor cart, then you should be able to describe your niche as "construction workers who break for lunch on site" or "adults and children who need snacks while playing or watching sports" or "business professionals who like a light lunch to avoid being sluggish the rest of the day."

If you're a handyman, then your niche could be "the first-time home buying professional who doesn't have the carpentry skills to do light repairs."

If you've got a barber shop, then you should be able to describe your niche as "upscale luxury services for men who want a quick haircut during the week" and/or "a place young men can come to get the trendiest hair cuts" or "a place where men come and get their haircut but spend some time socializing." The latter is where you might add refreshments to your business model.

If you are a sole practitioner attorney, then your client may be "young professionals in traffic court who prefer most communication to be electronic" or "senior citizens who are victimized by online predators or need estate planning"

Knowing your customer helps you perfect your business model. As you decide what you are selling, all of your products/services and marketing efforts can appeal to this customer. Sure you may expand to other markets, but start somewhere strong. Make money. Perfect your niche so your customer can celebrate your unique services.

STEP 5: Identify your niche with one sentence.

WHAT ARE WE DOING?

This is my rail against the so-called mission statement. I love my formal education, but I have to push back on this business plan/mission statement world we live in. In a microbusiness, the mission is: We are selling THIS and charging THAT to make money. Period.

I will challenge you to declare "what you are doing?" versus "what is your mission statement?"

"We sell coffee."

"We sell lingerie."

"We sell food and drinks."

"We sell hot air balloon rides."

"We sell legal services."

"We sell educational tutoring."

"We sell sightseeing tours."

"We sell pots and pans."

The key thing to remember is that you are always selling something. Never lose sight of that. If you are not selling, then your business is not thriving. Do not get into the weeds of the beautiful prose of a well-written mission statement. Those aren't for microbusinesses. Those are for businesses that are positioned for big investment or initial public offerings (IPOs).

Even after years in my fledgling business, I took a lot of entrepreneurial classes that allowed us to spend hours crafting our mission statements. While having coffee with Nancy, one of my very successful and favorite mentors, I shared my new and eloquent mission statement. Like skeet, she shot it down and said, "Listen, I'm just not that smart. What are you selling? And how much does it cost your business to make it?" Actually, she was wicked smart and extremely successful. I could not answer that question. I was embarrassed. I had fallen so far down the rabbit hole of all of these small business "classes" that I lost sight of what I was selling.

You don't need to be fancy. You don't need a slew of polysyllabic terms to tell you what you are selling and how much your products cost you. Don't overthink this. Stay focused.

STEP 6: State in one sentence what you are doing.

NO MANIFESTOS, PLEASE

If you went to college or business school or took entrepreneurial classes, your first inclination may be to write a business plan. Well, you aren't in school anymore. There will be no good grades for a useless book report. Instead of writing such a thing, build a website.

There are many user-friendly online template services where you can try to build the website for your business. It is the new brick and mortar. Instead of writing a pie-in-the-sky plan for a dream business, launch the business. Write the words you want your customers to see. Who are you? What are you selling? How can I reach you? Put it out there! I guarantee you, it will take hours to come up with the first image for the homepage. The first image you want your customers to see is so important, you will have an exciting time selecting from an infinite list of possible photos or drawings.

Look at 20 websites that sell what you are selling. Make notes about what you find most attractive about the sites that you like best. Is it the bright colors? The simplicity of the website, perhaps? After you've studied your top five, turn the computer off and write the headers, then words for your website.

Some of my favorite website builders are Wix.com, WordPress.com, and 1and1.com. Most of these sites come with stock photos that you can use if you don't have your own images. If you don't have a computer, then use your public library. If you feel too computer illiterate to build your site, then find a family member or friend to build it for you. To further customize the site, consider purchasing stock photos. On the Internet, you can purchase high-resolution, high-quality photos or illustrations for dollars instead of hundreds of dollars. This is a huge equalizer that allows the smallest firm to look as professional as the big boys. My favorite sites for photos are istockphoto.com, shutterstock.com, and dreamstime.com. It makes sense to pay a few dollars for strong images. The pricing structure determines how you will be able to use the images. The Web is getting more sophisticated. You don't want to just bum images from search engines. They are developing ways to block reposting of stolen images.

Selecting the domain name and tying the website to the domain and the public launch can be daunting tasks for those of us who aren't computer geeks. The exercise is much easier now and worth the angst to learn and complete yourself. It's also a much better use of your time than the manifesto. Besides, good paying customers like good, honest websites.

The only reason to write long narratives about your business is when you are specifically asked to do so in order to achieve specific gains for your business. Often, for example, a potential client will want to know about specific skills and services. At this time, you can spend time creating a document that addresses their inquiries or concerns. The goal is clear: new business.

One thing that is certain about a business is this: The more you succeed in growing, the more you will need to provide information, forms, and data to scale up. You will have plenty of opportunities to write long narratives about your business, its vision, and its goals. The difference is that when you are finished writing that "business plan, " you will submit it to a specific third party for a specific return. The return will be a permit, a certification, a prequalification or at best, a contract.

STEP 7: Commit to creating a solid attractive website instead of writing a business plan unless requested by a very specific third party for a very specific return.

BEING TRANSPARENT

Everything about your business should be clear and easy to find. Prices or price ranges should be clear with minimal effort. Gone are the days of "call us and we'll let you know" or "it depends." In today's marketplace, I will look for a company on my tablet or personal computer. If I'm not clear on some sort of pricing and an approximate location of this product or service, I'm going to select the next company in that category without batting an eye.

I met a wonderful young lady who sold delicious handmade tea blends. I was trying to find her business so I could order more tea. I found references to her business on Facebook, but no phone number. When I finally got her number from a friend, she said, "We don't post the phone number because we believe serious people will email us." Huh? I told her, "If I fell down a flight of stairs, I'd pass three more types of tea before I hit the ground." I won't try to find her like that again and she probably lost three other customers with this cloak-and-dagger strategy.

Every business needs a website, even if it is only one page. It is the industry standard now. If you sell food, your menu should be on the site. If you are a dry cleaner, your prices should be on the site. If you do lawn care, your site should say something like, "Prices start at $20 a week." It's no longer the case that you can provide just enough information to make customers come to your business. People now expect all of the information to be available prior to entering the shop.

If your customer base is young, then they expect you to have many of the following social media and Internet links promoting your microbusiness:

Figure 1:

Put a phone number on everything—but not a toll-free number. A long time ago, a toll-free number implied an established business. Now it conjures images of oversees call centers as well as impersonal and automated responses. Unless you have a restaurant that takes orders by phone, put your cell phone number on your microbusiness website and printed materials. Understand all of the calls that are coming in. Early in your business you are the main person who can answer every question in a timely manner. You can also solve problems right as they occur.

STEP 8: Be transparent in your promotions with prices and contact information.

LOCATION! LOCATION! LOCATION!

Where you launch your microbusiness is everything. The guiding principle of real estate is location, location, location! You have to be where your customers are, period. Finding some little free location that is hard to find and has limited places to park is not going to compensate for foot traffic. It doesn't matter how great your product is, new customers will rarely hunt for your space. The flip side is that many microbusiness owners just don't have the credit or the capital to move into a highly trafficked area. This is where you get creative.

If you've followed our steps so far, you are getting to know your customers, and how far they will go to buy your product or use your service. If you can't identify a more choice location than one with challenges, then be prepared to double down and then some on the marketing. You may even need to make the hidden location part of the mystery and fun.

But what if you don't have money for ANY location? Then you want to test your concept on the go. If your goal is to get into major sports arenas, then start selling your product at amateur league events. Start with a vendor cart. Create pop-up retail shops that are temporary locations. Participate in Flea Markets, Fairs or Festivals.

There are ways to do small launches before a big one. But there are also ways to negotiate a good starter space in a decent location.

Look for vacant storefronts in your desired location. Do a little research. If the building has had a long-time owner, you may be able to negotiate a really good starter rent that could escalate later at an agreed upon rate. This owner may be glad to cover his building costs and simply have the space occupied. But someone who has just purchased a building will most likely not negotiate with you. They have a mortgage to service. They will need everyone to pay the market rates that they told the bank they would seek.

Don't be afraid to approach a landlord directly. Understand that vacancy hurts everyone: the landlord, the surrounding businesses, and the residents in the community. Your microbusiness idea has value. If you can talk directly to an owner of an empty space, you may be able to negotiate something valuable for both of you. The fact that you will improve the interior of the space with your labor and materials is of value, too.

STEP 9: Secure the ideal location, if not permanently, then on a temporary basis via flea markets, pop-ups shops, etc.

DON'T BE A STRANGER

As an entrepreneur, you cannot hide. You want to be on social media. As people love your business, they want to love you, too. There is a false narrative that people don't interact as much as they used to. In fact, these new customers interact a lot, just in a different way. You should have a profile on the World Wide Web. This means you, not just your business.

The type of business you have may determine where you should be first. If you have a white-collar business, like accounting, management consulting, or optometry, you should have a professional profile in LinkedIn. Even if you don't connect with your customers/clients, your presence on the site with connections to colleagues shows that you are a valued part of your industry. You may also consider developing a Facebook profile page. You don't have to accept clients and customers on your personal page as friends; but if you are the head chef of a cool pastry shop, people will want to "like" a public profile page.

No matter what industry you are in, you should have a Twitter profile. As you grow your business, you learn that almost everyone is on Twitter. I had one for years before I understood the value (a generational thing).

But Twitter is a real chance to follow those people and businesses that share information relevant to you and allow your new fans to connect with you immediately. Perfecting this two-way relationship will allow you to really promote yourself and your business to people who are directly interested in you.

I strongly recommend an About Me page on About.me. This page only requires one photo image to represent you. It is a chance to add one quote about your life philosophy and links to your social profiles. This site helps build your online profile.

The main reason to have a social media presence is to allow people to vet you relatively quickly with your own customized message. New customers like friends more than strangers. What comes up if they put your name in search engines? This is an opportunity for great facts about you to appear. This is called search engine optimization. It takes a lot of work to get an unknown entity to the top of the search engines. But these steps are a good start.

STEP 10: Don't be a stranger. Build social media profiles on About.me and Twitter at least. Consider LinkedIn and Facebook, as well.

CHAPTER 2

GET TO WORK

REHEARSE AND SELL

One of the fun things about owning a microbusiness is that you make all of the rules. How are you going to greet your customers? What does your business pitch sound like? Don't make the mistake of thinking you've got it all clear in your head so you will be fine. You will only be fine if you practice.

What is the phrase you use to answer the phone? It should be short and sweet, but informative. "Hello! Johnny's Restaurant." And when you answer the phone, SMILE! Believe it or not, you can "hear" a smile on the phone.

What is the opening line of your business presentation? You can't just say, "Thank you for having me." You must have an opening line that is welcoming but catchy: "Today, we will introduce a new strategy for a more promising outcome."

You need to practice these lines and presentations to your friends and family. They will make the natural facial expressions, good or bad that you want as feedback. In the end, you want family and friends to smile and nod. This also gives them a chance to feel helpful without lending money or lifting boxes. Do the presentation in its entirety in front of others. I encourage you to do it more than once.

Practice makes perfect. Never use handwritten notes. Ever. If you have a slide presentation, then each slide should serve as a prompt for your speech. If you have leave behind materials, then pass them out at the end of the presentation. You don't want to bombard people with information they will naturally read while you are talking.

If you have a retail business, have one of your friends simulate walking into your store. What will you say? The first comment is the greeting. The second comment promotes the sale. "May I help you find something?" or "Make sure you look at our clearance table," or "We just got our new spring dresses in! Would you like to see them?"

Respect this process enough to rehearse your strategy. This is the first impression you will make with every new customer. You want them to stick around.

STEP 11: Rehearse your sales pitch, your phone greetings and your presentations. Make sure they are pleasant and engaging.

LIGHTS! CAMERA! ACTION!

Do it. Do it now. You have defined your business; you have business cards; and you have a website. Now it is time to market the business.

Our microbusinesses cannot roll out huge media campaigns on TV, but we still can roll out big. The key is to have the nerve to stand where people need you most and hand out a quick promo card to those people. Being creative about that location is going to give you an edge. Think about people who have a problem to solve. For example, courthouses are filled with people who have violations to pay. I personally have been fined $600 for the lawn not being cut on my vacant land. I saw people outside of the courthouse passing out postcards for gutter and downspout repairs. I was desperately looking for someone who does lawn care. My online searches found lawn care services that did not come as far as my community. The courthouses in your town, city or suburb are filled with people with very clear problems.

You know your customer, right? Where is she located? If you are selling dresses, you should have promotional cards at the clubs where these ladies party! This is where they look around, see what everyone is wearing and decide they may want to up their game. Don't just go to one club. Go to all of the dance clubs in your area! This is your version of saturating the market for your microbusiness.

Professional marketing outfits will tell you that people who hear of your brand seven times in a short period of time will retain your message in long-term memory. When time to recall your brand, i.e., when looking for lawn care or buying a dress, your business will come to mind early.

Promote your Facebook page or website to all of your friends online. Your friends already have images of you stored in long-term memory. They can immediately push your product or service to their friends electronically. Don't rely on word-of-mouth or postcards alone. In these modern times, people grab their smartphone and expect information to be readily available. Once they recall your name, they are looking to the World Wide Web. If you aren't there, you don't exist.

If you are stuck on passing out cards and promoting yourself on the Internet, this is where you want to engage younger family and friends. Many people will stand in front of the courthouse for you to pass out 500 promotional cards. You can get promotional cards for as little as $20. Two of my favorite sites for microbusiness are:

OvernightPrints.com
Vistaprint.com

If those don't work for you, find your own source. The only rule is, don't hand out crap. Do a professional card. Don't be tacky. This will be the first impression of your business. Don't blow it.

STEP 12: Get promotional cards to circulate in places where your customer frequently visits and pass them out!

SWEATING PAYMENTS

You must get comfortable asking for your money. If you have a consulting or service business, often the pay comes later. Don't let it be too late.

After I got a few substantial clients, I thought, "We will soon be rolling in the dough!" We started managing bigger clients, with downtown offices and administrative assistants! For some reason, this metric meant arrival to me. They have big offices; they have big staffs; and they have hired me. Ergo, I will soon have big offices and big staffs. This, I guessed, would be by association. I put on my best outfits and spoke with my best diction. I didn't want to appear needy. This is the Exclusive Club of wants--not needs. I will make sure not to appear desperate, as if I don't belong. I won't sweat these small invoices. I want to show these downtown groups that I am a team player. We will sort out money later, but for now we will have big meetings and lay out big plans. I am one of you now. I have seen the movie "Wall Street".

I had to laugh as I wrote that paragraph. I was as serious about that philosophy as I was about marrying my 8th grade boyfriend. I am sure, however, that no businessman or woman taught me that school of thought.

Part of this lesson came from good old-fashioned home training. It was simply rude to just ask for your money. It was also crass to demand payment. This works at the family picnic or amongst a group of college buddies (perhaps), but this will absolutely fail in business.

What I know now is this: Learn up front how your clients pay their bills. Ask these questions early while everyone is still friendly. Often, the bigger the company, the more rigid their process. Do they need all invoices in by a certain day? Do you need to enter your invoices into their complex website system? Does one individual cut their checks? If there is a process, ask about it at the time you are signing the contract. If the person you are talking to doesn't know, it's a red flag. Know that this person focuses on sales and not the complete relationship. It's not the end of the world, but it is something to be aware of from the start.

Try to befriend the person who cuts the checks. Don't pour it on too thick. A thoughtful jar of peppermints to the accounts payable team goes a long way when you are picking up your money. People remember kind acts and pay those people first. It's human nature.

A cool way to get your money is to have a third party from your "team" call to ask for it. This could be a spouse, a mature relative, or a good friend.

Someone needs to call the appropriate parties as a representative of your business. Consider compensating them with a success fee. Everybody will win.

They need to ask remiss clients on a regular basis what is required for you to get paid by a certain date. When you are a small business, it can be better that this call not come from you personally. Then your slow-paying client won't be able to make it personal. Your Accounts Receivable representative is simply doing a job. You can even follow up with your client, noting that your team is not getting a clear answer.

When possible, build penalties into your contracts for delayed payment. Understand that if you've got to do this often with the same client, then this is NOT a good client. You have to strike a better deal with them, or let them go. Another option noted later in this book is THE COLLECTOR. Keep reading.

STEP 13: Learn how your clients pay their bills. Pay attention to their payment practices. Give a thoughtful gift to the Accounts Payable team of important clients.

ORDERS NOT INVENTORY

You think it is a good idea, but are people going to pay for it? You do not want to spend a lot of money on a product that you are not absolutely sure is going to sell.   Don't make the mistake of ordering a huge amount of items hoping to save money based on the quantity discount.   This move will help your supplier's business, but it could kill yours before you get started.

Whether you are selling food or other products, you should invest in the samples being conscious of the time and money needed for small production runs, based on actual orders from paying customers.   Of course your microbusiness will not make as much money in the beginning, but it won't lose as much as it likely will if you order supplies that your customer base won't buy.

A smart and lean microbusiness does not carry a lot of inventory.   It is also smart enough to adapt immediately to stock more of what is selling and less of what is not. Within a reasonable amount of time, a great owner gets rid of inventory that is not selling.

Don't assume that it will regain value if you just give it more time. That would be akin to selling '70s fashions in the '70s and then waiting for 30 years for that fashion to return. Only then would you be able to sell some of those items for more than you paid for them. Of course, once you factor in the present value of a 30-year-old dollar and the cost of storing those items, you've likely lost a lot more than it was ever worth.

STEP 14: Do not invest in inventory. Invest in samples and then orders. Have a plan to scale only when the item is a success.

SIX WAYS TO GET PAID

Once you are in business, you will realize cash flow is just like blood flow.   You won't live without it. The slow killer of microbusiness is limiting the ways you can receive money. Businesses that require "Cash Only" are a dying breed. Personally, I avoid cash-only businesses. I can't track my spending that way. Also, as a woman, I don't like to carry a lot of cash. More than $30 in small bills seems excessive to me. I'm only buying mints and coffee at that point. I expect people to accept debit cards for my purchases of $10 or more. You want seamless and fast ways to get paid. The more your customers must struggle to give you money, the less satisfied they will be.

Cash flow is also relevant with accounts payable and receivable. You want to pay your suppliers fast. You want to receive refunds, etc., right away.

I recommend that microbusinesses place their main accounts at the big banks.   Your additional accounts can be in community banks that solidify relationships, but you need a lot of support. The big banks have it.

When you are sitting or standing in front of your customer, I recommend you have at least four of these six ways to get paid immediately.

1. **Cash** – The old standby currency. Note: this means of payment is decreasing every year. There is a lot of room for theft and error with cash, too.

2. **Debit/Credit** – Your bank account should come with a business debit card. You may obtain a credit card based on your personal credit history, but the debit card is mandatory. People can refund your business directly with ease with your debit card.

3. **Electronic Check Drafting** – Although decreasing in use, if you decide to accept checks, make sure you have the attachment to your point-of-sale machine that swipes the check immediately to deposit the money in your business bank account. This will reduce fraud.

4. **Mobile Credit Card Reader** – These little devices (e.g. Square or ROAMplay) attach to your smartphone and read credit cards with a swipe. Of course, you should have a credit card reader in your store if applicable. When on location, you can accept payment on the spot.

5. **Big Banks Online Pay** – The big banks allow you to pay and receive payments with only email address. This is very fast and makes people feel safer by not having to share financial information.

6. **Online Merchant Payment** – This third-party payment method is used primarily for online businesses. Third-party payments allow customers to feel safer because they know the business has no access to their financial information. The biggest provider to date is Pay Pal, but Intuit, WePay and others are gaining market share.

Do the research and learn the associated costs for these payment receipt options. Because you already know who your customer is, you will know their preferred methods of payment. Do this now, before a customer walks away from you because they don't have cash. You need to maintain cash flow. There's a big difference.

STEP 15: Establish at least four of the six ways mentioned to accept payments.

E-COMMERCE, eBAY, ETSY, etc.

If you are selling tangible products in your microbusiness, you should strongly consider an e-commerce website. These sites are customized to display products and receive money for said items. A basic e-commerce site only costs a few dollars more per month than a standard site. If you have a micro-budget for your microbusiness, take your own photos of the products. This is where you can make money without having to toil for it. But make no mistake: you will have to promote your site.

One way you may drive customers to the site is having promotional cards on hand where you are selling the products. A nice photo of the products and the website allows people to re-order items and share the information with friends.

If you want to sell items to an already established online audience, consider larger merchandising sites like eBay, Overstock and Shopify. These auction and online sites allow you to sell your products to a mass market. Familiarize yourself with the rules of selling your products. There are limits to the quantities you can sell and there are fees, too.

The obvious advantage is they already have a lot of potential customers looking to purchase items. The disadvantage is you will not be able to automatically retain information about your customer and you are listed as an anonymous seller. The transactions are practically anonymous. People pay through the site, and the funds are not released to you until they receive their purchase. You won't be able to market to that person directly. You can't efficiently build a customer base this way, but you can get a sense of the demographics of your customer.

A tremendously growing online marketplace is Etsy. This is a site that focuses on unique handmade items or one-of-a-kind vintage items for sale. It is like an online craft fair or online flea market. Unlike the previously mentioned auction sites, this one allows you to create your own visually attractive e-store. You still can't readily retain the customer information, but they can follow you. If your business turns out unique, handmade goods, then you should definitely put some or all of your items into your own Etsy shop. When this book went to press, it cost $.20 to sign up on Etsy. You've got $.20, right? If you're serious about your microbusiness, then spend it to open an Etsy shop.

There is a lot of information online regarding this topic. Familiarize yourself with this industry. Check out the sites and see which one works for you. You need to get your items for sale online. If not, you are leaving money on the table. We don't do that.

STEP 16: Create your own e-commerce site for your tangible products. Educate yourself on the auction sites and Etsy to see if any of them fit your business model.

BIZ TO GO

For business models that are more service-oriented and less about tangible products, consider some mobility still. If you have an ice cream shop, selling those items online might not make sense. You aren't going to outperform the big boys in that space if your flavors aren't very unique. Same goes for a nail salon. Your fingernail polishes will not be cheaper than big box or department store offerings, let alone Beauty.com. Some microbusinesses are using creative and innovative ways to get around.

If you want to test your retail concept prior to investing in a long-term retail lease, consider a pop-up shop. Many commercial landlords are considering temporary leases. It allows them to improve cash flow (over zero), maintain foot traffic to the building, and maintain curb appeal. One-to-three month leases are great for seasonal shops, testing the market, or simply not being tied to a permanent retail space. I have seen really nice pop-up art galleries, maternity stores, and candy shops to name a few.

Another way to create a "biz-to-go" is by putting your operation on wheels! There are some creative businesses rolling around in conventional bus and van conversions. I have seen manicure/pedicure small buses that come to your location for parties and bridal showers. I've seen recreational vehicles (RVs) converted to clothing stores and shoe boutiques.

A very common business-to-go is the food truck. They have the luxury of going to where the customers are.

You have already done the exercise of knowing your customer. Now determine if it is better to go to them rather than have them come to your location. Remember the cost of leasing a space for one year could be more than the cost of a van converted into your mobile business. Be creative!

STEP 17: Determine if your business is better as a mobile or temporary retail operation instead of a traditional retail spot.

CHAPTER 3

DO THE RESEARCH

COUNTING COINS

When I started my business, I did my little spreadsheets. My customer projections were directly exponential. I would get more and more customers every month. I would need more supplies, a little more labor, but I would make a lot more money. It was as if my business was in a vacuum. The way I wrote my numbers, it wouldn't matter what the weather was; I was going to grow. The truth is, nothing happens that way. I was in real estate during the real estate collapse of 2007. I pulled out my business plan for a laugh as I cried because I was losing everything; yet the spreadsheet said I would be rich by now.

The problem with this traditional projecting required by banks and other potential money sources is that it does not help you actually operate your microbusiness. The trick is - understand your numbers by the day and by the week. If you're running a restaurant, or retail shop, you may even want to look at your numbers by the hour. This will help you understand what hours are profitable for your operation and whether any of your opening hours – for example after midnight or before 6:00 a.m. – are costing you more than is being earned in those hours.

You don't have to look at all of the numbers every day, but you have to understand what revenue you need to hit every day in order to pay all of your bills. If your business is a daily operation, you will learn what are your best and worst days of the week. You will learn your seasons and you will be able to say, "When it rains, we lose 24 percent of our revenue."

A lot of good software systems tell you what your actual performance was in short order. It is essential that you start your business with the correct industry software. Do not open your business thinking, I will add this software later. Start with this software. If you have to side hustle to earn the dollars to get the software, do it.

Your business is your car. Money is the fuel of the business. You have to know how much gas is in the car at all times. You don't want to run out of either at an inopportune time. When I would run out of money, it was like running out of gas on the highway. I incurred a lot more losses through the bad planning by being caught off guard.

Now, I know how much it costs to run my business. My business is very seasonal and has very long sales cycles. I can see a drought six months in advance. It took me six years to understand that I needed to look at my cash flow trends. Don't take that long while growing your microbusiness.

STEP 18: Get strong financial software tailored to your business category. Track your spending and understand your required revenue on a weekly basis.

HAND ME DOWNS TO GET UP

If you are bootstrapping, almost none of your first items should be new. That is not only a mistake, but it's almost unattractive. If you ever need financial assistance (and most of us do), a ton of shiny new items will not make you look fiscally responsible.

Many businesses start up everyday and, for many reasons, many businesses fail. You need to get your supplies, equipment and/or location from the failures. When opening a restaurant, you can often get used restaurant equipment for as little as 10 cents on the dollar. If you are starting a food truck, get a used food truck. If starting an office space of any kind, paying for new furniture is a sin. You must get most of these items used, if not for free.

Always look online for deals on the items you need--used! Craigslist's "free" category is always a great place. Remember: if you are responding to a free-items ad, answer fast and offer to pick up the item(s) immediately. If you see a closed business in your neighborhood, contact the landlord/management of the building. Often these items have been left behind and are now a nuisance to the building. A quick offer of a small fee and fast removal can lead to great reward. It costs a great deal of money to dispose of furniture.

The rule is: don't haggle. Free is free and cheap is cheap. Remove all of the items you can from the premises if they are free. You can determine highest and best uses later. I've been on both sides of this equation. When I'm giving furniture away for free, the most offensive thing someone can do is come by with an inspector's mentality. You can take the item or leave it, but I will not submit to an interview past the description I've put on Craigslist.

> **STEP 19:** Make an itemized list of what furnishings you need to start. Proceed to finding the majority of these items online for free or extremely discounted.

THE PRICE IS RIGHT

Pricing your product or service with the right margins is critical to success. I have seen so many business fail in this effort. The key thing is that most categories of microbusiness have a pricing formula for success. If you don't take the time to research and understand these numbers related to your business, then you are being unintelligent and preparing yourself for failure.

Do you know that there is an annual coffee shop convention in America? If you are opening a coffee shop, you should really find your way to attend one or at the very least, get as much information as you can from the sessions of previous years. They have an industry specific formula for the success of a coffee shop. It includes everything from foot traffic to the cost of coffee beans to the size of the space.

If you are making a product that you plan to sell, pricing is a customized solution. I strongly recommend you read "The Makers," a book by Chris Anderson. It goes into a very deep dive of the new manufacturing industry revolution. There are very detailed strategies around pricing. Frankly, I have been in business a long time and because I have always had service businesses, I did not fully realize how to price a product.

If your microbusiness is centered on consulting, then pricing your services should be based on the value you are providing, a number that should exceed your costs. Therein lies your profit. If your business is as a life coach, then you don't want to say: "I charge $75 per hour because that's what I'm worth." You charge $75 an hour because you can show statistics that a year of life coaching can save thousands of dollars in mental and medical health bills from not pursuing a smart path.

If you are a personal trainer, you would value your services in the same way. If you are a marketing consultant, then you are offering to reach thousands or millions of potential customers in the marketplace for your client. You would propose, for instance: an increase in sales is probable with the likelihood of x-percentage of TV (or online) viewers actually purchasing goods. This would justify your consulting fee.

These are a few examples. The key is to understand your pricing. You cannot just charge what someone else is charging. You don't know what their expenses are or how they came to those numbers. Your numbers should be similar to what your industry charges, but they have to make sense for you in your city and with your customer.

STEP 20: Research the successful pricing formulas in your industry and determine a good price for your goods and services. Make sure to build in room for operating costs and profit.

PUSHING PRODUCTS

Whether it is food products, clothing, or some wonderful gadget you have made, there is a very specific methodology to rolling out these items to the marketplace. You have to price these items correctly from the beginning in order to succeed in your microbusiness. Take the time to do real calculations on your food or product costs. Then make sure you factor in all other costs and a respectable profit. Skipping over this very important exercise will kill your business from the start.

You already know your customer; you know how much money your customer has to spend on these types of items. Now, you want to measure your product against those in the marketplace.

Figure 2.

PRODUCT EXAMPLE: Food Cost is $1.50

Veggie Sandwich

	Restaurant A	Restaurant B	YOURS	Restaurant D
Vegetables	5	6	6	7
Bread	Bought	Bought	Homemade	Homemade
Price	$4.00	$5.00	$6.00	$7.00

In my example the food cost is 25 percent for all of the restaurants. That is in line with the food industry standards. You want to make sure your customer understands that your bread is homemade. Because that matters to your customer, right? Now, are the vegetables fresh? Are your condiments homemade, too? If they are, promote those as well. Your customer should understand why they are paying $2 more than the sandwich down the street at Restaurant A.

Are you selling clothes? Are the fabrics natural? Is all of the manufacturing done locally? You should make sure to put your information forward. Your customer should be able to see these facts on your website and in the information around the store.

As your business moves forward, you should always be looking at ways to reduce your costs. Can you source your materials locally? Can you order materials in larger quantities to save money now that you understand your demand? If your product is comprised of six main products, then make each part unique and special when possible. The remaining parts should be as inexpensive as possible.

STEP 21: When pushing your products in the marketplace, make sure you promote the unique and exceptional attributes of your offerings. And identify ways to reduce the costs of your products.

GET WINNING DOCUMENTS

If I could do it all over again, instead of blindly submitting proposals and other documents, I would have gotten my hands on some documents others had done that had successful results. Who can't pass a test when they have all of the answers?

If you are starting a consulting business, you will have to submit proposals for your work. The truth is, different industries have different standards for success. If your documents don't look "appropriate" the content won't matter much. You want to get hold of winning documents in the industry. This isn't cheating. It is understanding the game you are playing.

For example, my firm bid on work with a housing agency for years. We never made the short list, and I could not understand why. Finally, a colleague gave me a copy of a winning bid from three years earlier. My team's responses looked like grammar school textbooks compared to the clinical document before me. We had used 12-point fonts; they used 9-point fonts. We had overused clip art and useless photographs. They had emphasized cost savings, efficiency, and experience.

I was embarrassed that I thought our responses were meaningful. I re-thought our entire approach and rewrote all of our promotional pieces. The next time we responded to a request for proposals, we won.

Don't obtain the documents through stealing or spying. These documents are often available through asking or finding them on the Internet. Often completed projects are in storage, waiting to eventually be discarded. Colleagues will share information with actual values redacted. In this instance, you aren't looking for their actual costs; you are looking for style, format and content. Being successful in an industry goes much smoother when you blend into the industry.

What are the winning documents for your industry?

If you are in construction, obtain the documents of a building completed within the last five years. Your documents should look as professional.

If you are in the restaurant business, get copies of the monthly or annual operating costs/profits of a successful restaurant.

If you are starting a clothing website, identify 10 successful clothing websites that you like a lot.

If you are an advice professional (accountant, lawyer, media specialist, life coach, etc.), get copies of promotional packages and invoices of successful practitioners.

If you are an artist who paints on canvas, identify 10 artists whose career paths you admire. Review their websites, their biographies and the galleries where their work is shown.

If you will run a vendor cart, get copies of old but successful vendor cart applications.

If you plan to buy a lot of real estate, get hold of the documents of some of the last real estate projects you really admired.

If you will open a bed and breakfast, get copies of the bank documents, operating books and manuals of successful B&B operations.

There is no reason to spend valuable time blindly guessing how to pursue your goals. A far better use of your time will be to secure and review successful documents in the space. You don't have to copy them; the good works will inspire you.

STEP 22:   Obtain copies of winning documents in your industry.

BIZ BOOKS & BLOGS

There is so much good information out there; you are crazy not to do a little homework. Commit to reading at least one book on the subject of your microbusiness and sign up to receive the newsletters or blogs from at least four authors on the same topics.

You are reading a good book now, but read at least one more. I always refer a book to someone who asks for help starting a business. I have read quite a few. If they haven't read it by our next conversation, I won't help further. Answers for many startup questions have already been written. It's hard to help those who won't help themselves.

If you are serious about growing your business, you have a smartphone. There is always down time, whether you are in line at the grocery store or walking on a treadmill, there is an opportunity to read a little about your industry. Sign up for the newsletters and blogs of all of your suppliers. If they've got a sale or deal coming, you need to know about it first.

Along with your industry online information, sign up for blogs about entrepreneurship in general. We are a separate breed of people. The information in the good startup blogs helps us get through the tough times of angst and doubt. Coping tools and motivational tips are essential for a self-starter growing a business.

STEP 23: Read at least one additional small business book specific to your market or industry and sign up to follow at least four business blogs for entrepreneurship and your industry, too.

GET GOOD TV

Some of your research can be entertaining. There are some good television shows that deal with the inner workings of microbusinesses and small businesses. Aside from the standard interview shows where everyone is on their best behavior and passively/aggressively promoting their businesses, I like the shows that make the businesses better in one hour. I strongly recommend you watch these shows. Even when situations are overdramatized, there are some good lessons to be learned.

"The Profit" (CNBC) – A very successful businessman invests in a variety of businesses to turn them around.

"Restaurant Impossible" (FOOD) – A celebrated chef turns failing restaurants around.

"Bar Rescue" (SPIKE) – A very successful food and beverage consultant turns around failing bars.

"Restaurant Startup" (CNBC) – Two very successful restaurateurs decide if they will invest in microbusiness food concepts for growth.

"Tabatha Takes Over" (BRAVO) – A hair salon owner visits failing salons and turns them around in one week.

"Shark Tank" (ABC) – Venture capitalists listen to various business pitches to potentially invest.

"Consumed" (CNBC) – A documentary of various restaurant owners and the daily decisions required for success.

Commit to at least one episode per week of one of these shows. They provide some valuable lessons about the science of small business as well as the doldrums of working with family and friends. Even if you don't have cable TV, these shows are available for free or for a small fee online.

Entrepreneurship can be stressful. You deserve some entertainment and relief on this journey.

STEP 24: Watch at least one hour of microbusiness and small business turnaround TV a week.

CHAPTER 4

PEOPLE, PEOPLE

THE NAKED LADY & THE DRESS

My favorite African proverb is, paraphrased, "Never let a naked lady offer you a dress." What does that mean in bootstrapping your business? Don't take advice from people who haven't done what you are trying to do.

Starting your own business is filled with uncertainty. One of the most comforting feelings is to get advice from people you respect and even admire. The problem is that good people aren't necessarily good business people. And you cannot gamble when you can't afford to lose.

If you are going into a small law practice, then take advice from those who started a small law practice. Your uncle, the investment banker, may be really smart, but he doesn't know how to run a successful small law practice. If you are going to get a vendor cart, advice from a friend that owns a franchise restaurant may seem good, but it will never be as good as advice from a successful vendor cart operator.

The worst? Advice from career professionals. People who have spent their entire adult life working for someone else cannot tell you how to run a small business. They can tell you how they think others have run a successful business. But you will lose something in translation.

The second worst?   Someone who has never had a microbusiness or a small business, charging you thousands of dollars and/or hours of your time hosting workshops on small business. I'm not saying avoid all of these workshops, just make sure the people who you are listening to aren't "naked".

STEP 25: Identify 20 people who do EXACTLY what you are trying to do. These are the people from whom you should seek advice.

INFORMATIONAL INTERVIEWS

Don't guess how to start or grow your business. Ask someone who has already done it. Have informational interviews with top people in the industry. The trick is to meet the right people and make the interviews count.

An informational interview is where you talk to an important person in your industry. They should be stakeholders and/or decision makers in the business. The key is you are NOT looking for a job. You are just looking for information. We are hard-wired to think people who are potential competitors will not share valuable information with us. This is, in fact, not true. The more successful the person is, the more helpful they tend to be in your quest. You are not a threat. They have a solid customer base and their daily concerns are not going to mimic yours for a long time. You are someone that allows kind people to pay it forward. Not often is someone seeking his or her core knowledge. Their family is not interested; the staff just wants to know about right now. Their friends aren't interested. Even a reporter only wants the information about the story, very little more. But you will be interested in all of it. I have done scores of informational interviews seeking helpful details. I am no longer amazed at the amount of valuable information I've gained in this practice.

The Informational Interview Rules

1. When scheduling, ask for only 15 minutes of the person's time. (Work from his/her schedule; don't offer your availability.)

2. Communicate that you are entering the industry and want to ask questions about being successful in your endeavor.

3. Assure them you are NOT looking for a job. (Make sure to not ask for one.)

4. Do a great deal of research prior to the interview.

Sample Questions for the Interview

1. How long have you been in this industry?

2. How did you get started?

3. What is an average day like for you?

4. Is the industry different from public perception?

5. What advice do you wish you had when you got started?

6. What is your greatest challenge in the industry?

7. What part of your background best prepared you for this?

8. What was your best day in the business?

9. What was your scariest day in the business?

10. Are their certifications/accreditations that help?

11. What do you think is the future of this industry?

12. Do you plan to stay in the industry?

13. What technology do you personally use? (Smartphones, tablets, etc.)

14. How many hours do you work in a week?

15. Of people, product or process, which is most challenging to improve?

An important thing to remember is to interrupt the flow of conversation at the end of 15 minutes. Remind your interviewee that the allocated time is up. If he/she does not appear tightly scheduled, you can ask for a few more minutes or for one more question. This will show that you are considerate and respectful of others' time. Because you have been granted an interview, you are already ahead with this person. Don't lose that position. This is another way great mentor/protégé relationships are formed. In the future you may be able to ask that person for even more truly meaningful advice.

These are just some examples of rules and questions. Think of your own questions as well. There may be some good ones that emerge from your research. Asking specific questions that stem from specific knowledge will go a long way to maintain interest. Make sure they are not personal or around a scandal. You are here to make friends and get a sense of what you are getting into as a business

The basic rules of etiquette apply, too. After your session, send a handwritten thank you note. It need not be more than three sentences. Younger entrepreneurs may differ, but more elder ones--contemporary captains of industry, perhaps--are traditional. To them, an email seems impersonal. By no means should you text your thank you. That just seems dismissive and ridiculous.

STEP 26: Create a list of 10 people you would like to schedule informational interviews with in your industry. Meet with at least five of them.

THE TEST

When you need anything from anyone, there is almost always "The Test". The person seriously considering helping you will ask you to do something. Usually, the bigger your request, the bigger their test. In short, money follows the test.

When you ask someone for help they might say, "Call me next week to remind me." When you ask them for a meeting, they could say, "Send me a summary document for your project." When you ask them to be a member of your board of directors, they could say, "There's a book I would like you to read first."

The test is in your answer. If it's something that could be done immediately, you should have it done within 24 hours. If it's a one- or two-page document, you should not take longer than 48 hours. If they recommend a book, you should let your colleague know you have ordered the book within 48 hours and you should have read it within three days of obtaining the book.

This isn't college; you don't get a pop quiz or a makeup test.

You are being measured by your seriousness, by your responsiveness, and your willingness to go the extra mile. No one with authority wants to put their reputation on the line for people who do not follow through. In the eyes of stakeholders, if you aren't good for the little things, you will not be good for big things. Understand that if someone takes the time to test you on the follow-up, then you are closer to success than the alternative, the brush-off.

At breakfast, one of my mentors said: "You should read the book 'Liberal Bias.' It's really good." Ugh. That did not sound like fun. But as I'm walking to the taxi, I order this book from my cell phone through Amazon with one click. It came in three days, and I read it over the next three days. I found four interesting observations in the book I thought I could use in discussion. The next time we met, I mentioned some of the topics. He shared his opinions, and I knew he was pleased.

I use this method now. A lot of people ask my advice on starting a business. I recommend one of my favorite startup books based on the individual. When I see them again and they haven't read it, I'm no longer interested in helping. I can't help those who won't help themselves. For me, they are not the kind of entrepreneurs with whom I want to spend a lot of time.

STEP 27: Train your ear to listen for "The Test", and respond no later than 48 hours with a favorable action.

THE BENCH OF PLAYERS

For me, what hurts the most are the bad hires. I got this wrong so many times, I could barely admit it out loud. I read many books on the subject and I can only say that over time, I learned how better to fill a position. There was no magic answer. The only certain thing is that I wish I had spent more time developing a deep bench of players as I went through the bad hires. I would have let people go sooner, if I knew I could replace them faster and without too much incident.

First, I have to acknowledge my failure in these bad hires. I didn't respect my business enough to create a job description. I'm not some Fortune 500 company, right? Isn't it obvious? The job is to show up every day and help me. Since no one could read my mind, we had problems. Once I created a job description, I made better hires. People would show their laziness or disdain for work in the interview. It saved us all a lot of headache.

Still, putting a classified ad online for new hires or hanging a sign in the window brings both the desirables and the undesirables.

When you are building a microbusiness, it is difficult to hire a stranger who could be 33 percent or 50 percent of the entire team. That's a lot of eggs in one basket. Even when you are asking family and friends who may need a small job, you are sometimes scraping the bottom of the familial heap - someone you would have never selected.

If you need to add help outside of your family, find a few resources of people and organizations from which you can draw. Make friends with administrators of these programs so they will refer to you their best and brightest. In almost all communities, there is a job training center or some sort of re-entry into the workforce program. You want to make yourself known there. You meet with one of the program managers and say, "I'm growing _____ business. As we expand, we may need to hire _____ with specific skills. Do you come by those kind of people?" When the answer is yes, you've got a bench! They are training dozens or even hundreds of people and you get to choose from their best because you have created a great relationship with them. If you hire high school students, then get to know the local guidance/career counselors. They can refer decent students to you; instead of you taking a blind gamble on young kids. The same goes for local community colleges and trade schools in your area.

Sometimes these programs come with incentives. The programs could cover the first 90 days of the person's salary or you can be reimbursed for the employment taxes. Ask the program managers about these possibilities.

The key is to find pools of talent where people are already trying to better themselves.

STEP 28: Build a bench of potential players from where you can get strong referrals to work for you at your business.

THE COLLECTOR

In a microbusiness cash flow is everything. If you are in a service business where any of your money is paid later, delays in payment can kill your business. The people that owe you money rarely understand how dire late payments can be. Worse, if you are dealing with big companies, you can get stuck talking to Accounts Payable representatives who could not care less about your business. You are just another name on the list that will get paid sooner or later.

This purgatory can be very frustrating. As the owner of the business, you know how much is at stake with this slow payment. Your frustrations can turn to anger. Your anger can cause you to say things to clients you regret which can hurt your relationship. I have lost my temper with so many indifferent administrative assistants that held up my payments, I can't even remember them all. It was a problem until I got a collector.

Whether it is my office assistant or a friend, I have contracted individuals to simply call my client's office on a persistent and regular basis to inquire about payments. This is not about nagging. The purpose is to take the emotion and frustration from the conversation.

It is to neutrally gain the details for acquiring payment. You want to get just the facts. Your negotiator should be able to obtain dates or details of missing paperwork, etc. My fee with my negotiator is a flat rate, which they get paid when I get paid. When calling my client they would say something like: "Hello, this is Jane Doe from accounts receivable at Angela's Inc. I'm calling about invoice #1234 dated May 1, 2014 in the amount of $5,000. Sure, I'll hold." If the client's representative says "Can you call me tomorrow?" Jane does that without anger while I am somewhere throwing a fit because they don't have my money. Her neutrality will help us all get paid faster without the scorched earth I would have left had I made that call myself.

Keep in mind; if you continue to have a variety of problems collecting from the same client, you need a new client. It is a big world. Your business is too small to finance companies that do not do honorable business.

STEP 29: Determine who can act as your Collector of delinquent invoices when necessary.

PAYING TO PLAY

As you move forward with your business, you will learn the ugly facts of why it costs a lot to run a business. Whether you run a vendor cart or a one-man accounting firm, you will have to pay a lot of people. Every town, city, state or government has fees around recording your name and validating your business. When starting out, focus on the legal license only. Don't get distracted by all of the other dollar-based business certifications and membership offers that will come your way. Start with the basics, learn where your customers come from, then only join groups or obtain certifications that your customers require.

Then there are the politicians. It makes sense to know them, too. If you have a retail business or office location in a fixed area, it doesn't hurt to introduce yourself to your local politicians. Instead of getting the runaround from their handlers and gatekeepers, it might be easier to attend a fundraiser. For $25 to $50, you attend an event where your government representative is actually attentive and focused on meeting people in the community. You should know your representatives and they should know you exist in their community.

Unless you need zone changes or immediate remedies from your municipality, don't spend your early years building your political relationships.   Having introduced yourself at a fundraiser, you can easily approach them should you need something they are directly responsible for as your representative. The myth that they can make things happen for your business can waste a lot of your time. I feel the same about local community groups with membership fees, also.

Bootstrappers don't have time for community groups and meetings where people get together and pontificate about the way things should be in the neighborhood.   The entrepreneur's role in the community is to stay open, to thrive, and possibly hire more people.

STEP 30: Write down the names and contact information of the politicians in your area. Attend an inexpensive fundraiser and briefly introduce yourself and your business.

CHAPTER 5

DAY IN – DAY OUT

ACT LIKE IMMIGRANTS

We've heard this story hundreds of times. An immigrant comes to America, doesn't speak any English, has only a few dollars in his pocket and becomes a millionaire. There is no doubt this journey is not easy. But it does reflect some absolute truths. When you don't have the luxury of seminars, workshops, advice, business plans and long-range strategies, you find a way to sell what people will buy to make money.

Resist the urge to be distracted by all of the help of elaborate programming or complex business models to raise money. Keep it simple. When you find yourself considering a six-month course on how to run a business or getting another certification before expanding your business, ask yourself, "Am I moving away from the basics?"

You grow a business by growing a business. Don't stop and find a comfortable place to regroup. Immigrants have to stay focused. The goal is selling, growing, and earning enough to survive.

The immigrant model is:
1. Determine what you are selling
2. Determine how much people will pay
3. Make the transaction as simple as possible

4. Constantly find ways to lower expenses and increase revenues

5. Repeat

Each day you are in business, the solicitations to borrow money, join small business groups, hire subcontractors, attend awards dinners and others will increase. Ask yourself, "If I just arrived in America, would I do this?" The answer is almost always no. So, don't do it.

> **STEP 31:** Ask yourself, "Would an immigrant, *brand new to this country and* growing a business do this?" If the answer is no, don't do it. It is often a distraction from your core business.

THE BASICS

To some, this section may be obvious; but to many it is not. The basic operations of a microbusiness include the list below:

Operating Hours: Be open when you say you will be open. If you have hours posted on your door or on your website, they must be true. If you cannot commit to those hours, change your hours to "By Appointment Only." This won't work for certain retail businesses that rely on foot traffic. Don't be afraid to have limited hours. Most will patronize a business open every other day, but not a business that says it is open when it is not.

An Active Phone Number: If the phone number keeps changing or (heaven forbid) is disconnected, you will lose the customers who try to call. It screams instability and uncertainty. No one wants to put their trust in someone they aren't sure they can reach. If you are using your personal cell phone as your microbusiness phone number, pick a neutral yet professional greeting when you answer. Even though my business has a dedicated line, I answer my cell phone: "This is Angela." It implies you have called my direct line.

Keep Your Word: If you say you will call someone back tomorrow, do it. If you say you will cut their grass on Thursdays, cut it on Thursdays. If you make an appointment, be on time. No one, and I mean no one, cares about your personal situations and your tardiness. Once you are late, your credibility is diminished. If you are late twice, you're unreliable and unlikely to get more of my time and efforts.

Have a Uniform: You don't need the custom clothing of a 5-star hotel, but you and your team need to look as if you know one another. If you are performing lawn care, have your team wear jeans and the same color shirt. If you've got a food truck, do the same. For a starter restaurant, require everyone to wear black and perhaps the top waiters a uniform white shirt and black pants. Just agree on a uniform look.

Same time, Same place: With a mobile business, you have to frequent the same places at the same time to build a following. I can't tell someone how great you are if you are just driving around chasing dollars. Even if your food truck is on this college campus on Friday afternoons only, people will learn to anticipate that they can get perfect street food for the weekends on campus on Friday afternoons.

Business Card or Promo Card: If you can't place something IN MY HAND about your business with contact information, I will most likely not be able to retain any details about you and your business. These cards can be purchased for less than $25. I won't work with anyone that doesn't have a card. People will cut you some slack for style points, but regular paying people won't take you seriously without something.

I cannot tell you how many people make these basic mistakes. The thinking is, pay me now and I will do better down the line. The truth is people want to support local businesses. They also want to believe they are supporting a real business. Failure to have any of the above components will relegate you to small hustler status. Hustlers may make a few dollars, but they don't grow a business.

STEP 32: Perform all of the basics: Standard operating hours, business cards, keep your word, a uniform, familiar business practices.

THE NEGOTIATOR

Whether setting up your business or securing your contracts, you will have to negotiate your terms. You have to be very confident and secure enough to look people in the eye and say, "Yes, this is what I agree with." I have seen a lot of would be microbusiness owners get stuck here. People who have spent their lives working for others have a real hard time making the decision. Their natural instinct is to wait. These options should be taken back to a committee or supervisor for review and approval. If you have been institutionalized to the point you can't make decisions readily, you will have to become a Negotiator.

You have to be able to make decisions fast. You want to close the deal every time you are in front of a customer or supplier or whomever. The urge to say, "Well, I have to look into that and get back to you," has to shrink over time. When you walk into a meeting, you should already know your bottom line number. In other words, the maximum amount you are willing to pay or the minimum amount you will accept for your product or services. Every industry has a different amount of wiggle room. Feel free to negotiate back and forth, but you should get in the habit of closing the deal when you are in front of someone.

You want to end on a handshake and follow up with paperwork immediately if it is not a cash transaction. In less than 24 hours at the very least, you should follow-up with an email that restates the preliminary understanding.

If the deal is big and lawyers are involved, make sure your email includes your next steps. "It was a pleasure talking to you and establishing this new understanding yesterday. Per our conversation, we will perform [service] for [dollar amount] which will be paid on [date]. I will send a formal contract in less than one week." Make sure you keep your word regarding any transaction.

If you aren't a hardliner at the start of your microbusiness, have a close friend or colleague come with you to help you negotiate. I have seen far too many colleagues blow a deal because they are so uncomfortable closing a deal. They are either lacking the confidence to make a decision or they are hyper-paranoid that something moving fast will leave them being taken advantage of. The truth is, your first deal will not be as strong as your next deal. You gain expertise, you gain wisdom, and you gain knowledge. You can't get to the better deals without doing the not-so-good deals first. This is how the game is played. Now negotiate.

STEP 33: Learn to become a shrewd negotiator or bring one to the table when closing deals.

NO TO GOVERNMENT CONTRACTS

A big mistake for a little business is to go for the "BIG" government contracts. These contracts are gravy for a small business. First, you have to make sure you have a steady supply of meat and potatoes.

We see these huge contract amounts rewarded all the time in the media. The allure is awesome, why not go for this? The firm where you used to work got these contracts. Those people are as dumb as a box of rocks. You could do this so much more efficiently. Man, you and a couple of your colleagues were doing most of the work anyway! Right?

This is the mythological process:

First, you get the Request for Proposal (RFP) for said big contract. After you read it, get your entire team together and determine who else you can pull in to the process to meet these requirements. These early meetings will eat up valuable business resources and keep you from the basics, but hey, it feels right. This might resemble your past life of corporate strategy sessions and thus mistakenly feel like success. You'll also spend a great deal of time and money chasing this opportunity.

Now, if you can't bid for the contract by yourself, you can still become a subcontractor to a really large corporation. Government agencies' theory is these big companies *help* small businesses navigate these *complex* opportunities. OK, so it won't feel like help. It will feel like condescending, unending requests for information about you and your business that will never be read but need to be submitted immediately. You will be called into countless meetings with middle managers whose primary goal is to show busy-ness to their superiors. All kinds of decisions will be made without your involvement. The prime contractors' desire to maintain absolute control will leave you in the dark. But sometimes lunch is served. So if you complain, you're ungrateful.

Whether you bid as prime or subcontractor, if you're lucky, this process will take less than two years. With the staff changes, government elections and simple evolution of the world, this process can leave you in enough uncertainty to drain your business. Your team will inquire about that project. You'll have no real answers, which will help demoralize them. You can inquire about the status only to the annoyance of the government agency and/or the big firm's secretary. They'll tell you how busy they are and let you know what a pest you're becoming.

Performing the work then getting paid are other massive hurdles. Microbusinesses are the road kill on the government contract highway. Some small businesses can survive. Mid-size businesses fare better. Government contracts are really designed for larger companies.

Even if you win a contract, you will have lost so much in time and treasure you may never turn a profit.

STEP 34: Commit to building your meat and potatoes business before bidding on government contracts.

WHAT TO KEEP, WHAT TO LET GO

What you will soon learn about a legitimate business is the paperwork. Fear of not having proof of everything can cause people to hoard paper into a mental depression. Note to self, save all paperwork around the business fees. It's not only good recordkeeping, it makes filling out the paperwork the following year much easier.

Legitimate businesses have to pay fees and spend money. In order to pay the fees, you have to fill out more paperwork. To prove you have paid the fees, you have to save the paperwork. "Expediting fees" are additional fees to process your paperwork faster. To operate a legitimate business you may need a business license, permits, etc. Processing the paperwork can take weeks. To get out of the jam of waiting costs more and the fines for non-compliance are worst of all.

Each industry is different, but my advice universally is this:

WHAT TO KEEP:
Keep all business bank statements: If you are keeping them electronically, back them up as well as have them on your desktop. Do all business through these accounts.

Keep all credit card statements: Hopefully you are using more debit cards and keeping your debt to a minimum. But proof of payments is often required later.

Judgments and Legal Matters: Save ALL of the related information including all court documents, payments, communications, etc. Even after it is resolved, this can surface on your personal credit and in future court cases.

Tax Records: Keep in hard copy for at least seven years. I would say an electronic version of your tax records should be saved forever. (Make sure you confirm this recommendation with your attorneys and accountants.)

WHAT TO LET GO:

Client Files: After four to seven years depending on your industry, you should be able to let go all of the miscellaneous paperwork associated with former clients. Your online bookkeeping has the accounting and the bank records have the transactions. You can let this go.

Old Electronic Equipment: Download relevant files and wipe the hard drives clean. Get rid of these e-waste items: Phones, faxes, computers, monitors, etc. We tend to hoard these to obsolescence. They take up space and are less valuable each day.

Old furniture: Donate it to a local charity. If it does not serve your business it is burdening your business. A microbusiness is lean. A junkyard is a turn-off to new customers. If you get new shelves, bond with a local nonprofit and pay it forward. The networking and karma will bring you new business.

Old supplies: Resell or donate your industry specific items as soon as you stop using them. Supplies become obsolete fast. You hurt your business by keeping these items too long. If you can't find a charity, put them on Craigslist.com under "free stuff." I guarantee you, people will gladly pick up your items.

You see the trend, keep the money and legal records. Everything else needs to go if it is not serving an immediate purpose. Your business will be constantly evolving and growing. You must constantly rid yourself of items that are not directly growing your microbusiness.

STEP 35: Create storage systems for appropriate recordkeeping. Keep the important records around fees, licenses and money. Get rid of all FFE (furnishings, fixtures, and equipment) you are not using.

NOW MONEY

No matter what your business model is, you have to find a way to make "now money". Even on slow business days, what can you do to make sure some cash comes in? This is where you will see dry cleaners that sell lottery tickets. If you have a restaurant, you might invest in a vendor cart that sells some simple part of your menu at a college campus on Fridays. If you have a hair salon, you may negotiate to service the residents of the local nursing home every Tuesday morning. Your clothing store may need to sell hosiery or accessories that have a faster turnover than your regular priced items.

If your business model doesn't support that sort of add on, then you, yourself, may need a side hustle. This can keep your personal cash flow for existence while you are trying to grow the business. I can spend anywhere from one month to six months gaining a new client. Because I create so much text and data in my microbusiness, I actually enjoy building user-friendly websites. Just working with photos and images is a creative outlet and nice break for me. I make a little money while doing it. It is good "now money."

Most business books I have read gloss over this part. The chapters in the books imply you open the doors, greet the customers and then put the cash in the drawer. In truth, there are many slow days and times when you don't have money coming in. It takes a little time to understand what your customers want, what days they prefer to spend, and how much they are willing to pay. You will need other revenue streams than your dream business alone.

Building in some professional and personal "now money" strategies are important to keep your lights and phone on.

STEP 36: Incorporate professional or personal ways to make "now money" into your microbusiness strategy.

SOCIALIZING IS ESSENTIAL

If you aren't on Facebook, Instagram, Google +, Twitter, Pinterest, or LinkedIn, check your pulse to make sure you are alive. If your business isn't online it won't last long. Nowadays, everyone looks online for information about businesses. It is expected that you have not only a website, but a presence on social media. The more times your company is mentioned on different social media outlets as mentioned above, the quicker your name comes to the top of search engines. This is called Search Engine Optimization (SEO).

The most popular search engines in America are Google, Bing, Yahoo, and Ask. There are others but your goal is to be one of the top 10 companies that appears in the search in your area when people are looking for your product or services. Every year, fewer and fewer people check phone books for information. They pull out their smartphones. They type in "lawn care" or "hair salon" or "flower store". Their location is already in the phone. If you want their business, your name, location, and website link need to appear after the search.

Because you already know who your customer is, you can decide what social media to pursue first. If you will mainly work with white-collar professionals, you want to set up a company page on LinkedIn. If your clients are casual and social people, a Facebook page is easy to set up.

The goal is not only to have the client find your name and address. You want them to "like" your page or "follow" your page. Periodically you post information about your products, services, and sales. You also share valuable information in which your client would benefit. If you are a carpenter, your FB page could add tips on how to remove stains from coffee tables or DIY examples of painting furniture. Your clients will glance at your sales and tips on a regular basis and share them with friends. You are seen as a trusted expert and a trusted resource. Look at your competitors' social media pages. Understand how you can differentiate yourself from them. If you have teenage kids around your family or community, solicit their help. Posting information comes very natural to Millennials. Providing them with a little pocket change will go a long way to help promote your business.

It is the new world order, but a huge following can actually be more valuable than a billboard advertisement and far less money. The loyalty of "likes" and "followers" generates the kind of repeat customers all microbusinesses need.

This takes time. When you get the hang of posting good information, consider using websites that help you manage your posts. They are called Social Media Management tools. Two very popular tools are Hootsuite and SproutSocial. Or better yet, look at the search engines and decide which tool you want to use. The companies should be easy to find if they are any good, right?

STEP 37: Promote your business on social media outlets based on the profile of your customers. Maintain your search engine optimization.

CHAPTER 6

MINDSHIFT

TAKE YOUR PASSIONS

You've got to do what you love. It's cliché but it's true. There is a business model available for most passions. You can make an honest living and enjoy a high quality of life, and if you're savvy enough you can make a lot of money.

Do you know what you're passionate about? If so, good. If not, ask yourself these questions:

- What would I do with my time if I had $100 million and working for a living was not required?
- What would I be most sad about if I could never do it again?
- What did I have the most fun doing in the last three months?
- What would my family/friends think I'm passionate about?
- What was going on the last time I laughed out loud?
- What is the last thing I volunteered to do?

Most of the time, people associate passions with arts and crafts. That is not necessarily true. Through the questions above, I learned that I actually love doing business. I love the art of the deal. I enjoy responding to proposals, making presentations and most of all winning! I also know that I'm a tree hugger. I care deeply about nature, recycling and all that comes with it. So, I combined the two. I'm a professional Sustainability Consultant. I pursue large contracts to help businesses and organizations become more eco-friendly. I make a really good living. And I'm very happy.

But enough about me, what about you? Do you dare to believe you can make a living doing what you love?

Pursuing a small business just to get rich or to not work for someone else is a recipe for failure. Instead of getting rich, you will get depressed. You will not only work for someone else, you will be working for everyone else! Every customer is the new boss and you need his money. Instead of one boss you didn't like, you now need 100 bosses just to pay your rent.

STEP 38: Write down what you are passionate about. Base your business model on your passions.

DRINK BLACK COFFEE

The best advice one of my mentors gave me was "drink black coffee." To which I said, "No."

I was coming out of a large coffee chain with my polysyllabic coffee drink that took at least five minutes to prepare. I ran into my mentor, who always looks amazing and successful and feminine and fabulous. We had identical cups and for some reason, I said, "Hi, what are you drinking?" She said, "This is black coffee. What do you have? A lot of shit in your coffee?!"

Well, yeah.

She continues, "Look, you need to drink black coffee. You need to stop putting all that sugar and crap in your drink. Nothing good comes from that." Now I'm getting defensive. In my mind, I'm thinking, what does this have to do with anything? I look to you for professional advice and now you are ragging on me about the one joy I have in my frustrating quest-for-success day. This $4 cup of coffee with at least six ingredients is how I am defining personal success! If I don't have this, my life has no meaning.

What I said aloud was, "No, I could never do that." She said, "Yes you can, Angela. It was hard for me too, at first. Drink black coffee for five days straight and you will never put anything in your coffee again. You will actually start appreciating the true taste of coffee."

I was open to the possibility, because I knew how much it would simplify my life. Not only did I need my morning cup of coffee, but I needed it with the right flavorings, etc. or my day could not start properly. It was a handicap. If I started my day at some morning meeting, the wrong flavor of crème or lack of soymilk would send me into a mental tailspin.

So I drank black coffee for five days straight. Every day felt like a depressing closed-fist punch in the face. I only did it so I could explain to her in detail why it didn't work. That was seven years ago. I can't stand anything in my coffee now.

The moral of the story: you can make small changes. You can streamline your life and break bad habits by focusing on five days instead of forever.

Bootstrapping requires a lot of self-correction and self-motivation. I gave up cigarettes, soda and heavy pasta sauces using this five-day method. All of these things negatively affected my health and my performance during the day. Now I start every day with a cup of black coffee.

STEP 39: Figure out the crutch in your life that impedes your ability to be healthy, swift and earnest. Be honest with yourself. Live without it for five days.

THE ART OF THE SELF-START

As a business owner, it's all up to you now. You can both get up and get out everyday to expand your business or you can sleep in until someone puts you out of your home. Getting started on a regular basis is something you have to teach yourself.

This is hard for a lot of people. I have had many friends say, "Well, I'm going to ask you to hold me accountable." No to that. I will not assume responsibility, literally or figuratively, for getting you to run your business. This is a familiar crutch. Most of us were raised having someone else insist we perform our best. Whether it was a parent, teacher or a boss, we are accustomed to reporting to someone. It is their approval that has motivated us to do well.

Another way many put off actually accomplishing work is to get stuck in analysis paralysis. "I am working on it. I am weighing a lot of options." Or, "I have called a few people and they haven't gotten back to me yet."

There is no one else. You must set the timeline for work to be done and then do it. I don't have a simple remedy for this. We are all different and you have to look at your strengths and weaknesses to motivate yourself.

When I started my first microbusiness, I could blow off a whole week. I would go to the office everyday, but not get the hard work done. Now I do the hard work first. Often, 2 or 3 hours of serious concentration are all I need to resolve a matter. I write the report, call the people or make the final decisions early. This way, I have the mental freedom to take the rest of the day if I want to, but there is no slack. Every time I get a new contract, I give myself a bonus and buy something fun. It's my personal gold-star system.

The business won't run if you don't run it. If you need a boss then you can't be the boss.

STEP 40: Learn how to motivate yourself to work on your business on a regular basis.

THE KITCHEN CABINET

Entrepreneurship is lonely. All of the crucial decisions are yours. All of the crises belong to you. The buck stops here. You are scared to death that this last hiccup will kill your business. But you want to keep going. You have to have a kitchen cabinet of friends/advisers to get you over the hump. Here's the reality: This kitchen cabinet? They need to be entrepreneurs.

The term was coined regarding American President Andrew Jackson. He felt the office Cabinet of the White House was so ineffective that for political reasons he turned to an unofficial group of advisers and trusted friends. Though mocked by the press, they were very essential to the success of his first term.

We are the true job creators in the world. Unfortunately, we don't control the mainstream media, the politicians or the consumer understanding of small business. For that reason, you will encounter so many rude and ignorant people that will cost you energy, time and treasure, you won't believe it in the beginning.

If your friends and family are not already entrepreneurs, their responses won't help nearly as much as a group of peers who understand. Even when there isn't a clear solution to your dilemma, knowing this is a common occurrence takes some of the edge off of the problem. Your peers also have practical advice. They have had similar situations and can really add to the solution.

Four men and one woman comprise my kitchen cabinet. They all have had their businesses longer than I have. Our conversations usually consist of the joys and pains of microbusinesses. But one of my lifelong friends, Shawn, is notorious for letting me vent some awful experience where he says in the end, "Yeah, alright Ang. Just don't quit." I said, "OK." The first time he said that, I had been in business for two years. I had completely run out of money. I could not see my way past the next six hours let alone tomorrow. I just decided I wouldn't quit because I had said I wouldn't. I'm not sure there was another reason.

Your family and regular friends love you. They are going to recommend solutions that are familiar to them. They want to see you happy. They will tell you to stop this agony and get a job.

My mother supported my entrepreneurship, but it pained her to see me treated unfairly or poorly. She wanted me to have less stressful days and thought a job might be the best answer. I had to stop talking to her about my concerns. Neither of us was benefitting from it. I have learned to restrict family and friend conversations to personal matters.

My professional concerns stay with the kitchen cabinet.

STEP 41: Identify who is in your Kitchen Cabinet, a band of entrepreneurs you turn to for laughs, support and empathy.

SCHOOL OF HARD KNOCKS

Resist the urge to say things like, "I want to get a certificate in this first or I'm going to go back to school before I start my business". You will learn and you will pay substantial tuition to the School of Hard Knocks! Your microbusiness should be something you already know how to do. If you plan to go to beauty school and then open a salon, you are omitting an important step. You should go to beauty school and then work for someone else and perfect your craft for a few years before starting your own salon.

Don't get me wrong; I'm a big fan of education. Most of my team is college-educated. At one point, most of my team was not. There is a vast difference in the culture. What I realized, is that I prefer being surrounded by experts. I don't care about where you got your skills.

No matter how much education you obtain, you cannot be prepared for everything that may occur. What you can prepare for is the fact that a lot will go wrong. How you react to all of it is the core factor in how successful you will be. If this school had curriculum, it would include:

Keep Cool 101: The world is full of phone customer service reps that don't care if your problem is resolved. It's also full of customers who would gladly provoke you into causing yourself not to get paid.

Keep the Paperwork 204: Often, if you don't have the proof of everything, you will lose the money, opportunity and whatever was tied to what you could not prove.

The Money is Gone 210: The money you thought was coming isn't. The money that was there is not anymore. Learn how to suck it up and move forward.

Don't Cry Out Loud 305: Master the art of rapid blinking and controlled breathing as you listen to an indifferent clerical person, government official or politician explain to you how you are now losing all of this money. Their indifference will sting.

Keep It Pushing 410: Taking a hard knock and coming back the next day is the key to success. Develop actions you will take immediately to recoil from setbacks in your entrepreneurial journey.

All of the other incidentals on the journey to making a microbusiness are your events and yours alone. There will be triumphs and tragedies based on your industry and your personal expertise. You cannot take a class to assure that nothing will go wrong. A lot will go wrong. A class will test your patience and the tuition is extremely high.

Step 42: Understand there is a School of Hard Knocks. You will not be able to take traditional courses to avoid the hard lessons of entrepreneurship.

SIMPLIFY EVERYTHING ELSE!

Making a microbusiness can be exhilarating. All of the new information and the fact that you are your own boss becomes so gratifying that you will spend a lot of time learning about your business, listening to your customers and studying all of the new ways to make your business better, faster and stronger. All of sudden, you are more engaged in your life. The fact that you are pursuing passion and getting paid is a lot to comprehend or fathom. To avoid exhaustion, burnout, and overstimulation, you will do well to simplify everything else.

For a while, take the variety out of decisions that aren't important to your microbusiness. Instead of deciding what to eat for breakfast every day, pick a meal for the week and stock up. Do the same for the other meals of the day. Of course, you leave room for variety, but not having a plan is the worst thing to do. You want the basics in the fridge so you aren't trying to fill voids when you have worked on your business all day and forgot to get food.

Get a uniform for daily attire. The hassle of deciding what to wear daily takes time off of the clock. Like Steve Jobs of Apple when he made his decision to wear his signature Issey Miyake black turtleneck. It was a convenience that freed him to focus on more important things.

My basic uniform is a loose top, leggings, and TOMS© shoes. Only when I have meetings scheduled, do I pull out the fancy attire.

Figure out how much you need to live on a monthly basis. We are talking the bare basics like rent, car, utilities and (for me) cable. If you can, make sure that much money is in your personal bank account at the beginning of every month. Set your bills on an auto-payment. These are occurrences that you don't want to forget about when you are embarking on this new journey. Knowing this total expense and actually having that at the beginning of the month, reduces your stress tremendously while you are experiencing new stresses.

Determine the other tasks you scramble to resolve on a daily basis. Whether it is your workout routine, your social calendar or your personal relationships, encourage those around you to embrace this new simplification and routine you are creating. Those that support your endeavors will understand.

STEP 43: Simplify the routines in your daily life. It clears your mind to better grow your business.

LIVE LONG & PROSPER

The appeal of a traditional job is often the security. Mind you, those that need you to work there perpetuate that construct. You can achieve the same sense of security with a microbusiness. I'm talking about healthcare and retirement funds.

Healthcare in a word, Obamacare. If I wrote this book a few years ago I would tell you something different.

I spent the majority of my years as a microbusiness owner without healthcare. I have a pre-existing chronic condition called Sarcoidosis. This meant not only was insurance expensive, but almost every health risk was not included in my coverage. When my only child was entering grammar school, I got my only formal job. I needed the healthcare for my son. Getting my own, was a bonus. I chose to get a premium plan with a high deductible, since it was the primary reason I got the job. I kept a high deductible because I'm optimistic. Healthcare was awesome. It does bring a great peace of mind. But not enough peace for me to stay at a job. When my son started high school, I quit. My ex-husband covered my son on his policy and I was uninsured for years. Aspirin, wine, sleep and hope became my healthcare plan.

When America passed the Affordable Care Act or Obamacare, I signed up. I purposely sought the same premium plan I had at the old job. It is so affordable I can barely believe it! You can now get some kind of healthcare, whether a lot or a little. Roll this cost into your operating budget. You need the peace of mind of decent healthcare to run your microbusiness.

Retirement savings is the American way so I won't rail against it. A strong nest egg is comfortable for the soul in this uncertain world. So save some of these earnings. I know some friends and colleagues that won't leave jobs they hate due to the pensions and 401K savings. I ask a simple question. How much retirement savings would you like to have right now to feel safe? $250,000? $500,000? Millions? Most people don't have a real number. They just feel like steady savings is better than no steady savings.

I say know this number. Know how much it takes to make you feel secure. Get a financial planner to tell you ways to get to that number. I'm talking about one conversation, not a new codependency of a new consulting relationship. I put away money in clumps. I'm not good at weekly deductions and such. If I have a really good month, I take some part of that success and save it. But that's me. I have a number in my head that makes me feel successful. I'm moving in that direction so I'm good.

STEP 44: Secure healthcare coverage and create a retirement savings strategy to give you peace of mind.

CHAPTER 7

THE TEAM

PICKING A PARTNER

If you go it alone, it's a lonely small business. If you have a partner, make no mistake, it's a marriage. You can tell pretty quickly if this marriage is going to work. I had been in business about five years when the capital ran out. One of my options was to get a business partner.

My Partner:
It happened pretty fast. My company and I were just featured in a national magazine. It was good to be me, in public. I was asking a former coworker of eight years to come work for me. As a die-hard optimist, all I remembered was how smart she was. Sure she was kind of lazy and focused more on being cute than getting work done, but I had hung out with her and found her knowledge behind all of the slacking off quite endearing. Arrogantly, I felt with my leadership, she and I would work well together. Rather than just work for me, her new husband would put up her money to invest in my firm and become a part owner.

Bonanza! I'm going to get the capital I need to stay open and I'm going to work with my old friend. With her on board and taking the advice of my current CFO, we started letting go of the little clients. We would have the capital to pivot to the big leagues. What could go wrong? Everything.

She had no intention of working hard. She didn't in the eight years I worked by her side in the past and she didn't now. Her new husband didn't put up the money. He gave ten percent of it. Because their marriage was new, she didn't want to rock the boat with this failed commitment. Within two weeks, the memory of all of her shenanigans as a coworker came rushing to the front of my mind. In a larger company, the team could absorb her slack. She complained that this was too much work and she thought it would be more fun. She was also tired of me asking where was her portion of the money. Her husband would let her know and then she would let me know! Really?

I had already introduced her to our largest client. She had met the team. As a partner in this firm, her slack was an anvil in a two-woman balloon. We were falling fast.

Six months later, the company had fewer clients, less money and fewer people as some great employees left after I brought a nightmare into the business. We signed a one-page document where we agreed to just dissolve this arrangement. She told all of our old coworkers that she may have to sue me. Of course, there was no lawsuit. There is only egg on my face from choosing to believe in my own arrogance; that I could make a known personality into a different human being. I now refer to the experience as the hurricane. Here, you either fail or rebuild.

When you decide to choose a partner ask these questions:

1. Do you have the same goals? If one of you is in it for the love and the other for the money, you will have problems.

2. Do you have the same work ethic? Are you the type to stay up all night to finish, while the other will put this off until later?

3. Are you both punctual? If only one of you values others' time, this will get old fast.

4. Do both of you need this business to succeed? If one needs it to survive and the other has another primary source of income, you will not be equally yoked.

5. Have you worked well together before? If not, it's like getting married when you haven't dated. It could work, but it's a long shot.

The best way to start a partnership is to plan an exit strategy. Decide, in the beginning, to reassess the partnership at a certain point in time. Whether six months or a year, agree to honestly determine if you want to go further together or not. Each partner should have a way out. It may be a small buyout clause with a one-page document, but make sure it is legal with some sort of financial consideration attached.

STEP 45: Decide if you really need a partner. If so, agree on a point in time to assess if the partnership is working and the appropriate exit strategy if it is not.

CROWDSOURCING

Only a few years ago, it took a lot of money to get a decent looking business up and running. Now you can hire people from all around the world to accomplish things you need. This phenomenon is known as "crowdsourcing". You can source services form around the world. What's great for you in the global marketplace, is you can find really good quality services for a lot less than you could even five years ago.

To get a professional logo, have a well-written press release, create your Facebook page, build your website, write some of your blog entries, design your brochure, enter data, proofread documents, create your policy manual, etc. you can find someone from around the world to create the item for a small fee. If you have a few dollars to spare, I recommend you look into some of these professional services rather than doing each of these things yourself.

There are countless websites with crowdsourcing staff available for hire. After using a few of these sites, you may even offer your services for hire. It could be easy "now money." They are easy to use. I am addicted to three of these five sites for microbusinesses. They are:

LOGO TOURNAMENT – http://logotournament.com/ They have thousands of graphic designers on their site ready to compete to give you the best logo for your business. For a few hundred dollars and active participation, you can get over 100 personal ideas to choose from.

GURU – http://www.guru.com/ They advertise they are the largest crowdsourcing resource on the internet. Most professional office services that can be performed online can be solicited on this website for very reasonable prices.

DESIGN CROWD - http://www.designcrowd.com/ The talent on this site is primarily graphic artists. This site emphases the creation of logos, brochures, business cards, t-shirts and websites. Their pricing structure is different but still very simple.

UPWORK - https://www.upwork.com/ (Formerly Elance and O-desk) They have tens of thousands of freelancers that perform an infinite amount of services for hire. You create a request for services with a detailed description and many people bid on the work from around the globe. Most freelancers have been rated by other users and have portfolios online to aid in your decision to use them.

FIVERR - https://www.fiverr.com/ This site is where many will do almost anything for $5. How fun is that?! From having a dog hold a photo of your company logo in a photograph to a banner to a 30 second jingle, this site can make your promotions fun!

Once you start crowdsourcing, you quickly realize there is no excuse not to get the materials needed to have a successful microbusiness. If you are serious at all, you have five dollars.

STEP 46: Use crowdsourcing to get the remainder of the items needed to have a successful microbusiness.

GETTING A GREAT LAWYER

First of all, I don't think you need a lawyer, until you need a lawyer. Attorneys can be expensive in general, but they aren't that expensive when being specific. That may sound cryptic, but it is very simple: when you get in trouble, you need a lawyer. Look at the trouble, and get an attorney with expertise in that area to resolve the problem.

To legally set up your business, you can often go directly to your city, state and federal websites to get the paperwork you need. You can also go to collective websites like Legal Zoom if that would make you more comfortable. Some states require a registered agent. I have had attorneys for that service, but I recommend that in your first year, you put yourself in that position. You need to understand all that the government requires of your business before you hand that off to someone else.

Personally and professionally, I have six different attorneys working for me at the time I am writing this book. My firm has a tax matter with the IRS as a result of a mistake I made years ago in the business. I have an attorney that specializes in tax law dealing with it. He has made me understand this situation in simple terms. I no longer have night terrors.

I have a piece of land that keeps getting heavy fines from the city. I have another attorney that lives at the city's courthouse. All he does, day in and out, is deal with city fines. Everybody there knows his name.

Due to a death in my family, I have a probate attorney.

My son and I agreed to put all of our assets in a family trust. I have a trust attorney. The list continues.

When I started my microbusiness, I thought one good small general practitioner would be my attorney. I was willing to pay a monthly retainer because that is what I learned in school. Do not do this. I know all attorneys have access to the same legal documents, but experts and specialists are better for your little business. Often, they charge a few hundred dollars to get you in and out of a situation. This is all they do and odds are, you are too small to have done any real damage.

I have found my best attorneys online. I lucked up on one good referral, but a website I have grown to trust is Avvo. http://www.avvo.com They have a wealth of attorneys in their database with specialties and ratings. These are attorneys who have taken the time to present themselves in the marketplace. They have identified their specialties and been validated by clients.

Once you call the attorney and schedule a preliminary meeting, have all of the documentation regarding your dilemma with you. Make sure you have already made a copy for the attorney to keep. This will save you a lot of money because that first consultation is often free and if you're prepared, you end up getting some free advice. If you hire the attorney, they have all of the information you have. You can get back to your business and they can resolve your matter in short order for a smaller fee.

On the flip side, if you come in scattered, panicked and unprepared, you can be an unattractive client. It will take more time to deal with you and thus cost you more money.

STEP 47: Get a good lawyer only when you need one.

DIGITAL ASSISTANTS

Technology has allowed us to have real assistants from around the world or virtual ones in our hand. As you grow the business you can hire traditional assistants. For starters, every microbusiness needs a smartphone. You should get your first digital assistant from the phone.

Whether it's Siri from the iPhone, Google Now from Android phones or Cortana for the Windows phone, your phone should be one of these brands or an equivalent with the digital assistant.

It is completely unacceptable to say "I don't use that type of phone." The technology is the best tool for a micro business owner. For young people this is a no brainer, but for some of us older people, we are intimidated. When I got my first tablet, I stared at it for 15 minutes. I had no idea how to turn it on, charge it, or use it for that matter. Now I ask this assistant to do a series of tasks:

> "Remind me to pay the insurance bill every three months."
> "What is 175 divided by 50?"
> "Send a text to my accountant."
> "Wake me up at 6:00am."

"Look up the address of my client."

"Add my appointment to the calendar."

"Call my son."

"How much is a flight to New York?"

"What's the weather for tomorrow?"

"Set a timer for 35 minutes."

My digital assistant takes no days off and rarely misunderstands me. I started my business before the invention of digital assistants. This invention removes at least $25,000 from your microbusiness' expenses for a live assistant. I know this for a fact.

Learn how to synchronize your business email, your business calendar and your business contacts to this phone and a desktop computer or the Cloud. Depending on your computer literacy this can take an hour or a day. Whatever it takes, you must invest the time to utilize this modern assistant.

STEP 48: Get a smartphone with a digital assistant. Synchronize your email, calendar and contacts. Back them up on the Cloud.

COUNT ON THE ACCOUNTANT

All the books and blogs tell you to find a good accountant. I haven't read a story on a good method to find the right accountant yet. I recommend that you look for a great accountant AFTER you have all of your records in an online software tool. I have had my business on the same tool for ten years, so I don't know the variety of online tools in the marketplace, but there are quite a few out there.

Do the research. Even if you are dedicated to your smartphone or the public library, take the time to look up the right software for your business. Some of the tools focus on specific industries. The more information you can find about a customized software system for your money, the easier your life will be.

For the first year of business, enter your own data into the software system. You must understand your finances before your turn this responsibility over to anyone else. Your finances on your records should match your bank statements dollar for dollar. The easiest way to track your spending is to get a debit card with your business checking account and use only the banking debit card or written checks to do business. In these modern times, that is very easy to do.

Withdrawing cash and keeping manual receipts is not only messy, but requires a lot of busy work that slows you from growing the business. Taking a shoebox of wrinkled receipts and sloppy notes to an accountant will cost you a lot of money to have them sort that out.

If you are really disciplined, you can update your records every month and use a software tool that synchronizes with your bank account. Or you can be like me - I update my records almost quarterly, wishing every time that I did not put it off.

With all of your records online, now you can shop for an accountant. As a microbusiness, you mainly want them to file the appropriate taxes. You don't want them to "do the books". Once you have selected one, you can grant them access to your online accounts. They can make recommendations as to how to improve your recordkeeping, but you are not starting from nothing. You know your business.

I like cold calling from an online search, as well as referrals. Let's say that using the best online search engines, you come up with some accounting firms near you. I like this method because those companies online tend to be the most modern, the most progressive, and those actually seeking new clientele.

When you call, do you speak to a live person? Do they seem interested? Book an appointment. Prior to the appointment, you can give them access to your files with their email address. At the appointment, ask: "I have a _____ business. I'm looking for an accountant and I need to make sure I'm in compliance with local and federal filing laws. Can you help?"

Once they give you the sales pitch, ask "What filings does a business like mine have to comply with?" If they say anything like, "You tell me what you want me to file," run! You need an expert. You're not the accountant. Also, make sure your accountant has the professional authority to sign your tax returns as the preparer. You want a professional. Good answers should be specific: "You have to file, this, this and that." "The IRS requires this and our state requires that" "My fee is X". You want to know if your accountant will remind you of due dates or not. Good online accounting software will often remind you of legal filing dates too.

For microbusinesses, these fees can have great range. Believe me, the fees are smaller when your books are in order. I recommend you pay this professional at least annually. Mistakes with the federal government are painfully time-consuming and expensive.

STEP 49: Get a good accountant.

COVER ME

As America is a litigious place, people will sue you as sure as look at you. You will need insurance. The good news is, it is not as expensive as you might think.

Once again, I think online search engines are the best place to find specialty companies. It's easy to be "in good hands" or have someone "like a good neighbor" when looking for personal home, life and auto insurance. Now you have to find someone to insure your little heating and cooling business or your flower cart. Who does that? If you are following my action steps, you are already interviewing people in your industry, making new friends and acquiring mentors. Ask them for insurance representative referrals. It's a no brainer. You should shoot them an email. Asked and answered.

Often times you are simply carrying liability insurance. Unless you get into other areas like food and beverage or something that requires customers to use physical exertion (e.g. a gym), you are insuring against scenarios that rarely happen. If you've got a consulting service, you will probably have to have errors and omissions insurance.

When responding to Requests for Proposals you often have to provide a very specific kind of insurance for the project if your company is selected. Sharing that exact information with your insurance representative will allow you to avoid buying excess coverage.

You know you have the right insurance representative when you say, "I have _____ business, what kind of insurance do I need?" And their answer is either follow up questions about your business or "you need _____ and _____." When someone says, "I'm not really sure" or any equivalent of that statement, you should move on. There are plenty of experts that sell the type of insurance you need. There should be only one newbie in this conversation. And that's you.

STEP 50: Find the right insurance carrier. Get the appropriate insurance.

PLEASE, NO MEETINGS

In short, entrepreneurship is lonely. Many compensate their fear and trepidation of braving the new frontier by holding a meeting.

Stardate, 2012: There are eight of us. There is a big corporate table and I am telling you we look important. We are all sipping fabulous coffees or drinking bottled water with beautiful fruit plates and bagels. My friend, who we will call Gary, is about to explain why we are all gathered. He wants our help and support as he starts his new business. After his opener, we all go around the table, state our names, share our academic credentials and highlight our awesomeness. It's a scene straight from the movies.

For expediency, he could close this business now. I know it's not open yet, but this would be the least expensive route with the fewest emotional scars.

Why? Because Gary is not starting a business, he's building an expansion of a corporation that doesn't exist. Often, these kind of consensus-based startups are created by people that have been institutionalized by corporate groupthink for too long.

The mentality of a corporate person is to hold a lot of meetings, get superiors to approve time and travel for the meetings, document said meetings, plan the future meetings, get a line item budget for the meetings, develop subcommittees to meet outside of the meetings, and then meet about it. It is the same mentality as that of the lonely man.

In the beginning these meetings feel great! New relationships are forming and everybody is talking to Gary about his idea. All of these professional people are tossing out ideas, success stories and endless possibilities. These meetings feel familiar and safe. Even better, they are about a subject very interesting. By the third month, Gary still doesn't realize we have not done one actionable thing. I tell Gary I can't come to the meetings anymore. My [insert whatever here] happened and I will no longer be able to participate. One-by-one, the others peel off. This isn't looking like our group photo will make it to Fast Company. Food has been served. Time cannot be recovered. The sting of rejection sets in. Doubt rears its head. Gary reviews his binders of meeting minutes, notes, quotes and anecdotes. Somewhere in the paperwork, he comes up with the reason he's going to put this business off for right now.

Years ago, I would participate in a ton of these meetings myself. I wanted to be supportive, as I want people to support me. In hindsight, these sessions weren't helpful for general concerns. They work when you've got a very specific question you'd like a very specific group of friends to address.

Running a small business can be scary in the beginning. A small business owner has to make a huge mind shift. Consensus building for early business decisions is a sign of weakness in an already fragile situation.

STEP 51: Resist the urge to have a consensus-building meeting. Only have a meeting to solve a specific problem, not for ego boost and encouragement.

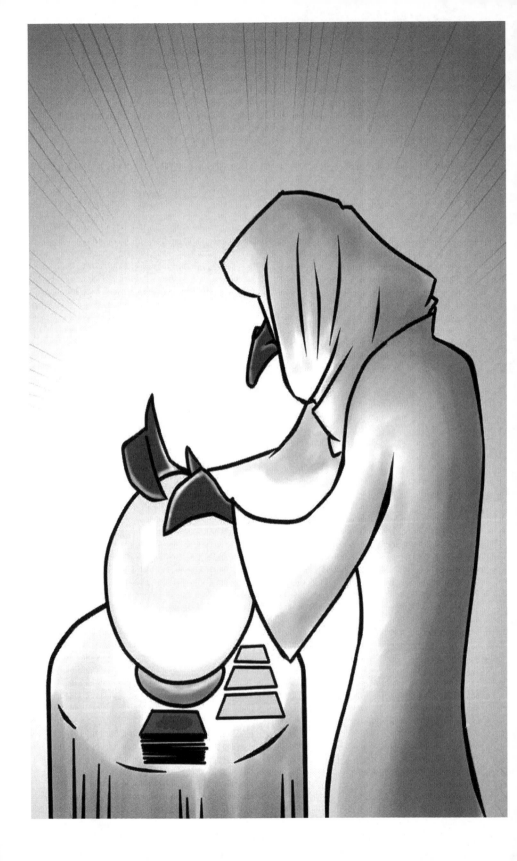

CHAPTER 8

THE ASSISTANCE

A GREAT MENTOR

There are tons of articles on the fact that you can always use good mentors. Very few of them tell you how to get them in the small business world. And even if you complete some informational interviews, those conversations don't automatically turn into relationships. Large corporations build mentor/protégé relationships into their culture to improve employee retention. Microbusiness mentors are obtained differently.

Know that people want to help. Someone helped them. They want to pay it forward. Established professionals that like you really want you to do well. It improves their karma. It makes the world a better place.

But don't confuse your mentor with your friend. Your mentor doesn't want the responsibility of making you feel better about being an entrepreneur. They don't want to hear your personal problems about your cash flow and how it is hurting your family. They don't want to hear about your ugly customer. They don't want you asking them for money.

For starters, I secure face-time with my potential mentors. I determine through our conversation if this person is interested in my business or me in a meaningful way. People tend to engage or disengage very early. If all looks promising, I ask if I may call on them from time-to-time for small pieces of advice. If they are receptive, I know we are off to a good start.

These are my rules of engagement:

Rule 1: My mentors have to have accomplished what I want to accomplish. No naked ladies offering dresses. (See Chapter 5.)

Rule 2: I can contact them to schedule coffee, breakfast, lunch or drinks. The more established they are, the more meeting bumps, cancelations and postponements occur. It is par for the course. I know I'm not a priority.

Rule 3: Rarely plan to meet more than four times per year. I usually meet with them less than that. I communicate more often with email.

Rule 4: Never ask an emotional question. I ask specific tactical questions. How can I decrease my costs? How can I better source this product? Can you recommend a patent attorney? How should I set my invoice terms? What is the best way to approach this potential client?

Rule 5: Always provide a handwritten thank you note with a stamp sent in snail mail. My mentors are older. I stay with tradition.

Mentor/protégé relationships are unique and individual. You may be able to establish one that allows for feelings and such. I would call that person more of a friend. I advise against it. These people have their own family and friends to embrace. You are one tantrum away from being avoided. Then all that good advice goes out of the window.

STEP 52: Create a list of desired mentors. Pursue relationships with all of them.

ACCELERATORS, YES OR NO?

Accelerators are the newest trend in promoting small businesses. Unlike standard entrepreneurial groups and meetings, these are formed with the purpose of actually investing in the business with the intention of "accelerating" the growth for financial gain.

Well, aren't they all for financial gain? Sort of. Entrepreneurial groups are usually limited to advice and study, but accelerators do a lot more. Investors looking for rapidly growing businesses run accelerators. These are usually investment structures that have a reasonably good business that would thrive if only it had a little more money and the exposure to the right opportunities for growth. Think of the TV show "Shark Tank". That program is about a group of investors who may add capital into your business, take an equity stake in the business and help you grow much faster than if you did it on your own.

While everyone can't get on a national TV show, accelerators are springing up in many cities. Usually each accelerator focuses on a specific industry. These investor groups are smart enough to know the industry they are in. Rarely do you find a one-size-fits-all accelerator out there.

So, yes or no?

It depends on what you really want to do with your microbusiness.   If your model is to grow by any means necessary, then it may be worth it to apply and try to get accepted.   If you plan to run a lifestyle business, meaning this is your livelihood and you would like to grow it your way, this may not be a good fit for you.   Many of them look for SaaS (Software as a Service) businesses.   Because these are online businesses, you can often apply to join accelerators in other cities.   If it's interesting to you, research them in your business category.

If it is a good fit, I recommend you hire a grad student or someone with investment knowledge to help you with your financial projections if this not your expertise.   The investors looking at potential businesses to join their accelerators are used to seeing growth strategies in very traditional formats.   A great deal of people try to get accepted.   Your numbers need to be realistic and plausible.

The truth about accelerators is that investors have opinions about the growth and direction of your business.   Once you've been accepted into the program, that investor's opinion becomes more than an opinion, it is the direction you will probably take.

A colleague of mine went through an accelerator. The relationship began with the investors taking a seven percent ownership stake. That grew to a 50 percent ownership stake. Expectations were made very clear. In the middle of the project, my colleague felt like he was really working for them. In the end, they sold the business for a lot of money. That worked for him. He was not passionately tied to the business. You have to decide, would that work for you? If so, go for it.

STEP 53: Decide if you want to pursue joining an accelerator. If so, do it.

THE INCUBATOR

Often times cities, communities, nonprofit organizations and the like want to spur small businesses in their neighborhoods so they take a huge space and form an incubator. This common space is designed to be cost efficient and collaborative. Entrepreneurs get to work and mingle around other entrepreneurs sharing resources and the like. The goal is to attract small businesses that aren't necessarily strong enough to survive on their own.

I think an average incubator can be a crutch and a bad incubator can be a killer. Before you consider joining one for all of the convenience, ask yourself, "Is this the best location for my business?" Don't ask yourself about the cost savings of the location because you will lose that value with missing customers. Before running your business from an incubator, you should be able to list five advantages for being there. Four of them should tie directly to improve business. Is it in a better location for your customers? Do they have speakers and suppliers coming to this facility on a regular basis? How many businesses like yours have been there and grown to acquire their own facilities? Does being located at this incubator provide discounts to services you frequently use, such as supplies and phone carriers?

A good incubator isn't trying to be everything for everybody. It has a focus on a specific industry. It has a strong online presence and a lot of good case studies and success stories. It has a calendar of events with topics and speakers that can advance your business.

Before you decide whether or not to be located in an incubator, you should already have the fundamentals of your business model thought out. Knowing exactly who your customer is and how you need to engage them should directly impact the decision whether to locate inside an incubator.

STEP 54: Ask the correct questions prior to choosing to locate your business in an incubator.

ENTREPRENEURIAL GROUPS

You have to watch out for these groups. It's my humble opinion.

There are few greater wastes of an entrepreneur's time than the small business group program. Some programs cost thousands of dollars. Some are free. Either way, they suck valuable time and resources from you growing your business. Just like those pills they sell on infomercials in the middle of the night for weight loss – buy this and your problems will be solved! The miracle promises are often the same. And nothing is really that simple.

Here's when they DO work: When you want to expand your contact list with other people that are in small business. It helps to have like-minded people to run your ideas past or talk to. These become your coworkers. You can't really hang out with people that work for you. You can't discuss financial concerns with them. Your family is tired of hearing about this business. These are your peers. We all need peers.

I'm speaking from experience. I signed up for so many of these things, you would have thought they were footballs and I was Peanuts' Charlie Brown. Maybe all of them aren't awful. But if I had $25, I would bet $25 on 95% of them being awful. The first group I joined was actually very beneficial to me. I met a lot of people that are still friends and fellow small business owners. The network of colleagues saved my business. The programs did not. I know now that I could have met these people directly. Those friendships would have formed organically.

The small business group scenario is usually one of two models:

A. One is the well-meaning social agency that has workshops to help your small business grow. Either it costs a lot of money or requires a lot of time or both. They ask you to expose the entire financial position of your business and family. Then they determine if they can help you. Often, none of them have actually run a business, but they'll have a certificate or degree in Entrepreneurship so it's OK. Many times these social agents have a grant to run a small business assistance program.

B. The other group is the big corporate organization trying to help the little guy. Often this model is free. This is usually the brainchild of their public relations arm trying to solve the problem of the company's image of crushing small businesses or not having enough diversity. They find some talking heads to lead the workshops. To sweeten the pot, there's mention of potential capital resources. Very few people really qualify for that money.

In both groups, they will tell you of some successful businesses that completed the program. I promise you, those businesses were successful before they walked through the door. You will also sign permissions for photo releases. Your smiling face, and perhaps your company's name in print, is what will feel good at first. But it's often a placebo. These well-intentioned instructors will say, "If you reduce your expenses and increase your income, you'll earn more money." Really? Had you not said that, I would not know that.

How do you determine if you should complete one of these programs? I told one mentor about these classes and she looked at me as if I had gone mad. She said, "Don't pay $50 for anything to grow your business where you're not absolutely sure you will get at least $51 back." I think that is good advice.

> **STEP 55:** Don't join an entrepreneurial group unless you are very sure what the outcome will be and it will indeed grow your business.

ASSIST AGENCIES & WORKSHOPS

[Heavy sigh.] Assist agencies are where a great deal of taxpayer dollars go in but very little assistance comes out. Often, they are nonprofit organizations with staff, classes and collaterals created to help small businesses. They can receive millions of dollars from the government, wealthy donors or fundraising events to pay staff and lead workshops to help grow small businesses. As always, there are exceptions to the rule, but in my twenty-plus years as an entrepreneur, I can only think of two assist agencies that were helpful, and I still would not recommend you go to those two.

What they offer is a series of one-size-fits-all workshops that are designed to help you become an entrepreneur or start a small business. The problem with the entire model is you don't become an entrepreneur that way. Making a microbusiness is analogous to becoming an athlete. Business is just like sports. Your skills only improve with consistent and repetitive action. You cannot take a class on running a marathon. A six-week course that reviews the regimen and history of Olympic athletes will not help you nearly as much as six weeks of actually running every other day. Even worse, the teachers of these courses are rarely entrepreneurs. It's akin to taking that same sports history course by someone who was never an athlete. It's a waste of time.

There's a promise of representatives that can help you and networking events to promote your business or even membership with other attractions. To me, they are photo opportunities and form-stack creations to show demand in the marketplace that allow them to renew their grants. Then the cycle continues.

The reason we are stuck in this business model for helping small businesses is because they are born from academicians. Some really credentialed people have obtained grants to "help" and they in turn hire some smart people to "teach us" something.

I push back on curriculum that starts with entrepreneurial classes. I think we startups would be better served with a track of courses that include business, finance and our core competency. However, school is for learning, so it's not that harmful. But these agencies that replicate school are a waste of time. If you find yourself drawn to attending one of these things, make sure you aren't just scared, that you aren't just seeking some external validation that you have to be able to find in yourself if you truly want to do this.

Just like the baseball player who stands there and swings at the ball 100 times a day to improve, you should make 10 cold calls a day or pass out 100 post cards to promote your business. This is a far more valuable use of your time. You will learn more about growing your business than you ever would at the agency.

Every now and then, the government or some foundation has funneled money through assist agencies that can benefit your business. You want to be established and seasoned enough to take advantage of those opportunities. That is later in the game. Now, again, waste of time.

STEP 56: Wait until you are more established in your business to join an assist agency. Do not sign up for startup workshops that are actually more of a distraction.

THE VENDOR FAIRS

As a rule, I'm not a fan of vendor fairs for microbusinesses. You have to really have the capital to make a decent impact with strong visuals and great giveaways to even get someone to remember your name if you invest in a booth to gain new customers. To me, fairs try to be too much to too many people. I have had a business booth at some vendor fairs and I have attended others looking for ways to grow my business. My conclusion is they are very expensive endeavors and there are really good questions to ask yourself before investing time and money either way.

If you are considering having a booth at a vendor fair, ask yourself, "Are the people scheduled to attend this fair your specific customers?" "What are the demographics of their audience?" If you are selling adult diapers, you need to know that this women's expo has a median age of 32 before you invest in booth rental. Your clients won't be there. But if you have a lawn care business that services a small area and that area has a homeowners' association vendor fair, it may be well worth your time to be there. Almost every visitor at the fair is most likely a homeowner and a potential customer, either individually or as a group.

A good rule of thumb is at least 75% of the attendees are potential customers. I just went to a small expo to pick up my packet for an 8K race I entered. All of the vendors selling running gear, shoes, t-shirts and headbands had my attention. One vendor was selling window replacements for homes. I averted my eyes. That was ridiculous.

If you are thinking of attending a vendor fair as a potential customer/attendee, it should be for the direct reason of reducing your costs. You should have a list of what items you use on a regular basis and what vendors at this fair can deliver a better product for you for less money. If you are thinking of traveling far to attend a vendor fair, make sure you have added all of those travel costs into your decision as to if this is worth it. If your travel, room and board costs $2,000, would it be worth it to possibly save $500 on an expense? No.

Leave those expensive vendor fairs to the big firms that can play those reindeer games. The best way to benefit from those events is to look online for the collateral (brochures, presentations, etc.) after the event. Obtain a list of vendors who had booths. Look at their websites online. If they have enough money to pay for a booth, they are likely to have a comprehensive web presence. Everything you need to know will be on the website. If you have any questions, you can call.

Now, I just saved you $2,000. You're welcome.

STEP 57: Determine if you really need to go to vendor fairs. (Probably not.) Use alternative methods to obtain valuable vendor information.

CHAPTER 9

SOME MONEY

CHEAT ON YOUR BANK

When you start your business or if you are in business now, you'd better have a bank on the side. Open at least two business bank accounts with two different banks.

Opening the bank account with my business' name on it was such a thrill. Creating my business plan for the bank and applying for the SBA loan was exhilarating. The branch manager knew my name and the tellers smiled every time I walked into the bank. This is what entrepreneurship feels like, right? I will be loyal to this bank until the end of time.

I started my business with a Small Business Administration loan. I received 25% of what I asked for. That's OK. I was approved and it was a signature loan. I have no intention to fight this *feeling* of approval of my community. Sure the math wasn't there, but this is just the beginning of my awesome new journey. My then accountant said, "They gave you just enough to fail." I proceeded to yell at him, "How dare you be so cynical! Why would you say something like that? This is something that happens in business and I can adjust." I refused to utilize his services again.

As math would have it, the money ran out. The bank branch that loved me didn't even know the difference. Once they closed the deal, my loan was actually managed by some far away people with a toll-free number. Their attitude was "hey, loan number 24503985, you missed a payment!" I entered the business death spiral.

Clearly when I started the business, I was creditworthy and so was my business. Had I developed at least two business-banking relationships instead of one, I would have been able to have at least one more conversation about my business growth with a friendly banker. Looking for a new bank when your relationship with your only bank is thinning out is too late. No bank really wants you when you reek of fear, desperation and actually NEED help.

The other reason you need more than one bank is simple. When you make a mistake with the government, they freeze your main bank account to get your attention. "What? My debit card didn't work? What?!" I said, at the office supply store. It's true, you can work it all out, but I had to pay people and I couldn't tell them my account was frozen. This is where corporate people cut bait.

I remember being in this situation and a client having mailed us a $5,000 check. New bank accounts have hold times. I need this money yesterday! Had I had another account, this would not even be a footnote in my life. Instead it's the time I had to borrow $500 from my ex-husband for five days. We both winced through it.

STEP 58: Open at least two business bank accounts at separate banks.

BUMMING MONEY

Sometimes, no matter what, you will need a little money. Your back is against the wall and in order to keep moving, you need cash. The truth is, you get by with a little help from your friends. Another truth, no one wants to loan money to people who need it.

Like the five stages of grief, you have to go through the five stages of debt.

1. Admit that you need money.
2. Determine exactly how much money you need.
3. Realize there is no debtors' prison. You can face your creditors.
4. Acknowledge what has to be paid now and what can wait.
5. Accept that you can get this money.

Money is attracted to opportunity. Smart money avoids problems. When you are up against the wall, figure out exactly how much money you need and why. It's a simple list:

Description   **Amount**   **Penalty**

Before you ask for one dollar, shrink the excess from your problem. Liquidate something. Eliminate another expense. Smart money won't support a businessperson that won't trim the fat. Call all of your debtors, acknowledge that you are aware of the debt and you will pay it. Many of these people will stop calling you once you have called them. The lack of constant calls about debt really lightens the stress.

Once you are clear on all that you still need, it's time to figure out how you can make at least twice as much. Most people make the mistake of asking people to pay for their shortfalls. Now that you have your head around the problem, you have to focus on shrinking the problem and building the next opportunity.

Everyone's different, but I've observed and experienced these successes:

- It's easier to ask family to cover a "growing" expense. Instead of asking for $500 dollars, ask can they cover the light bill for six months where you can pay them back in one year. Family often wants to help, but don't want to put money in your hands. The same $500 you would have paid for that expense, can now start paying an immediate debt.

- Have a massive sale or clearance. Have advance sales of services at a huge discount to get over the cash crunch. Holding inventory until the market rebounds can be suicide. Working hard for less money for the next few months is a valuable lesson. Offer the best deals to your friends and family. They have seen your work. They know it's a good deal. They want to help; but they want a value for their dollars.

- Borrow from your friend by running a huge promotion on something already successful. Only borrow the money for promotional material or direct supplies for this new wave of business. If you sell from a vendor cart, only borrow enough for food that you can immediately sell near a big event. You pay your friend back, and then pay down some debt. It's a short-term loan where you have a history of success you can easily replicate.

Microbusinesses don't need or want big loans. It may give you a false sense of security, but it gives you a real debt. If your business doesn't have a means to make fast money, it's not a microbusiness. It might be one of those college case-study businesses that have complex spreadsheets and projections that mean something to big bankers, but the rule of microbusiness is: If it doesn't make dollars, it doesn't make sense.

STEP 59: Determine how much money you need in crisis. Devise a clear plan on how much you need for your next "opportunity". List the people you know who have money. Start asking.

GRANTING WISHES

Business grants are sources of funding that businesses will not have to pay back. They are pools of money often created by governments and nonprofit organizations to help small businesses start or grow. Unlike a loan that you have to pay back, grants are like gifts of money. Friends who try to help you will tell you of all of the grants available for small businesses. Spending an extraordinary amount of time pursuing these "opportunities" is a mistake for a microbusiness. You are not growing a business; you are chasing money.

A smart microbusiness starts with a product or service and finds customers who will pay for the product or service. Of course a grant will help launch your business, but it won't make your concept more successful. It won't teach you the things you need to learn in order to grow and be profitable. It only means that someone in charge of giving out grants liked your idea and it fit their criteria.

Think of your most underachieving friend. This is the guy who talks an interesting game, but never gets to the finish line. He has an idea for a business. Now give him $5,000 to start that business.   Do you really anticipate a more successful outcome? No. It is just an outcome with a $5,000 grant as part of the story.

I know what you're thinking: "I could still use that $5,000!" Who couldn't? My point is, some of those grant applications are very time-consuming long shots. If you can apply for a grant in an afternoon, fine. Go for it. If it is a longer process, wait until you have proof of concept for your microbusiness and you are cash flow positive. Your employees can work and you will have the greater understanding of how your business is working and, most importantly the time to attract grants. But often these grants require microbusinesses to go to a social media site, solicit "votes" from their friends, and jump through several more hoops for the chance to get a grant. You would do better to ask a friend to support your business than waste that "ask" for a long shot.

STEP 60: Don't invest valuable time in early stages of your business chasing grants. Focus more on building a solid business.

CROWDFUNDING

This is a growing phenomenon where ordinary people like you and me fundraise for projects through online platforms. You have an opportunity to promote your product or event through text and video and create different "awards" for donations. The general public then reviews these offerings and donates money to the ones they support.

The most popular crowdfunding platform in America is Kickstarter®. Other popular sites are Indiegogo® and RocketHub®. There is so much information on these tools that I encourage you to do your own research for which site may be good for you to raise funds.

I have seen crowdfunding very successfully used for product launches. If you decide to utilize this platform to raise funds, I encourage you to note the following:

1. Understand the success fees and the rules of keeping the funds for your fundraising platform before you start a campaign.
2. Study successful campaigns with products similar to yours. Make sure your promotion is as interesting or more.

3. Campaigns with promotional videos no longer than 2 minutes are more successful than those without videos.

4. For every day of your campaign, you should have a different group of people you are sharing this campaign with online. Plan this before the start. Whether it is different groups of friends or different blogs, your outreach should be aggressive.

5. You should have already backed a few campaigns. It improves your profile, even if you only give $5.

6. Understand the success fees and the rules of keeping the funds for your fundraising platform before you start a campaign.

Remember that crowdfunding is best when you have a great offering for the donors. A new product often has appeal. A new restaurant or food truck can have a strong local appeal, too. It is something they would really want or want to see happen. The campaigns that seem to be merely fundraisers don't fair as well.

Read at least 10 blogs on successful crowdfunding before considering this as an option. I love the platform and I donate often, but I can tell when someone is simply fishing for money versus when I am supporting a great campaign.

This platform isn't suitable for every business model. If it doesn't make sense for yours, don't waste your time. Successful campaigns take a lot of time and planning. It may make sense for you to just work to attract more customers.

STEP 61: Learn a little about crowdfunding and determine if this makes sense for your microbusiness. If you use it, plan a thorough campaign before you launch it.

UNLOAD INVENTORY

One reason you may need money is because everything you tried to sell didn't sell. This is where you need to resist the urge to hold that inventory for a better day. Hoarding won't help. In a country full of instant gratification, the longer you keep items, the more likely they will lose value anyway.

You need to have a SALE. We have all seen those signs that say: "GOING OUT OF BUSINESS." If you provide a service, you need to put a promotion online with an email push to your customers for a huge discount if they utilize your offer within a certain amount of time. The best strategy is a huge clearance sale sign with a deadline for the sale to end. You want to create some urgency, and discount items enough to make an impact.

Discount the items that aren't moving in the store. They aren't good for the business anyway. This will make room for more of the items that do sell. If you run a restaurant, you make this decision everyday. Anytime you have to throw food away, you should reconsider having it on the menu.

This might seem obvious to some, but in my years of business, I have seen many business owners hold on to items they think will sell next season or when it rains. The ability to let go and no longer commit to failed ideas is directly related to being successful.

STEP 62: Unload inventory that is not selling. Discount it a lot to gain capital and free up space for better items. If you have a service, discount a popular item for a short time.

TIME FOR BIG MONEY?

The move from microbusiness to small business happens when you raise/earn larger sums of money. In a perfect world, the time to raise more capital is clear. You have bootstrapped your microbusiness and it is growing by leaps and bounds. You need real capital in order to meet the production demands from all of these customers. Or your food business is so crowded, you need to expand the space to stop turning away new business. You know the financial costs of your business products and services, you have weeded through all of the bad hires and your systems are near perfect.

There are countless books and financial advisers on how to grow a business at this point. I won't try to reduce this very important task to a few words. If you are running a successfully growing business, congratulations!

You will decide whether to look for an equity partner or debt financing. Equity is when people or entities put money in your business and agree on to become a percentage owner or owners of the business. Debt financing is borrowed money from a bank, person or entity. They do not take ownership, but most often require collateral or your guarantee to surrender something of value if you do not pay it back in the agreed upon time often with interest.

I will caution one thing, strongly reconsider raising money to turnaround a failing business unless it is accompanied with an expert equity partner. The person/people who take equity in your business are now part owners. They win or lose with you, so everyone has a reason to make this work.

I also caution raising money on speculation alone. If you think a bigger space will make more money than a smaller space or new decorations would attract new people, this is the wrong time to go for big money. You are not sure if that will help. Debt financing will aggressively follow you through life. Banks will seize assets and aggressively work to recoup their money. The penalties of debt are not worth the damages on speculation alone. I started my business with a Small Business Administration loan. I regret this. I had so much to learn and I was already in debt. I experienced everything I write about in this book, and the stress of a debt I struggled to pay is just one of those things. My bank was acquired by another bank and that big bank decided to call my little loan. In other words, they wanted full payment immediately. I didn't even know you could do that! It was a nightmare that took me seven years to resolve. Who needs that?

Everyone talks about how to get money for your business. Just make sure you are getting money for known business reasons, not just hope and ideas.

STEP 63: Only solicit big money when you are already running a successful microbusiness and the new money has a proven concept behind it to succeed.

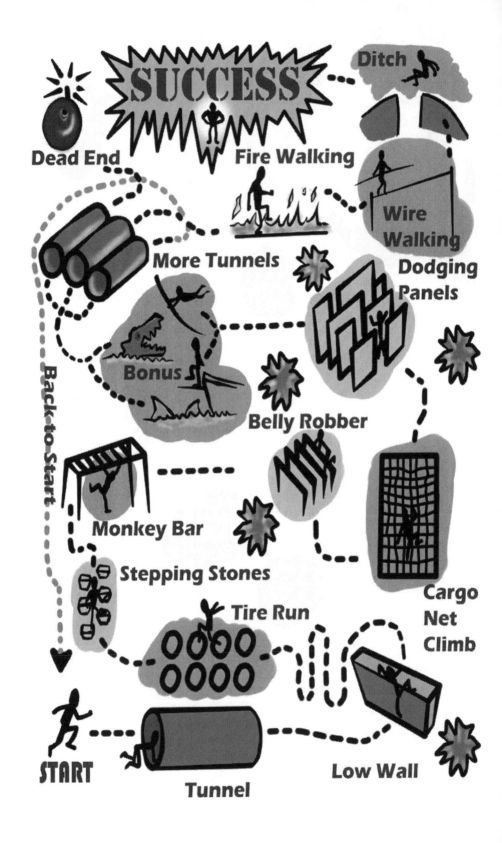

CHAPTER 10

THE HURDLES

THE SHUT OUT

Capitalism is mean. Business is a sport. Capitalists play to win at all costs. If you approach business as simply a socialized means to exchange goods and services, you are going to get crushed. A good business opportunity for you is likely a good opportunity for someone else. If you give a little bit of slack, the other person will try to shut you out.

If you have a food truck and you have finally found a good location, soon someone will grab that spot. They may have the political influence to ban you from it. If you have a small accounting firm that looks busy and successful, prepare for a similar business opening up in the same building when you were assured that there would be no similar leases. In any service company, some jerk will decide not to pay you the full amount, though you have performed the service in full. Or perhaps you've put together a team of small businesses or experts to pursue a large project--and that team then tries to cut you out of your own deal.

The good news is this doesn't happen until you are successful enough to have something worth trying to grab. The bad news is a few of these people will get away with their bad acts.

Sometimes you will have the right legal team in front of the right arbitrator to stop this tactic. Sometimes you will connect with the right authority who will do the right thing. Unfortunately, often times, these authorities will take the path of least resistance. Whether this works out for you or not will have nothing to do with merit.

As a microbusiness owner, you have to learn how to take these lumps and move on when the battle is cost prohibitive. Just know that as your business grows, you will have the resources and resolve to not be shut out of your worth. You will be experienced enough to spot an attempt to shut you out early. Then you can crush them.

STEP 64: Understand that as a microbusiness owner, you will be unjustly shut out of opportunities you deserve.

IT TAKES A THIEF

Bad hires can hurt your business. They cost you time and money for training or just adapting. But hiring someone who steals your clients and sets up his own business on your foundation can truly kill your business if you let it.

I've only hired two of these people in 14 years of being in business, and I have decided that isn't too bad. The first bad hire came as a referral from a former coworker. I had a bad feeling about her from the beginning. Call it woman's intuition, but I didn't really like her. My business was pretty new and I was having real money problems. I no longer trusted my own instincts. I was over a barrel with a very big client. So I hired her, effectively placing her as a bull in the china shop that was my client's location.

The first afternoon I stopped by her location and I realized she had opened up the electronic files dealing not with the client, but all of my company's invoices. In this moment, I knew I had a problem. She was far more interested in what my company was making than what she had agreed to be paid.

She was going to try to cut out my business and get this client for herself. I had already been managing this client myself for a few months and discovered that arrangement was not sustainable. But she was the third hire I'd put on this client. This was a nightmare. In the movies, this would be the point where the music crescendos. The loss of this huge client and the failure of my business quietly flashed before my eyes.

I was trying to find someone else to take over this account. Or at the very least, help me with other client concerns while I took over the management of the account again personally. My company was hemorrhaging money as a result of the issues on that account. More people had to have their hands in this particular pot than was originally planned. My CFO and I thought that the project was a real growth opportunity, but the client was sucking all of the oxygen out of the room. Ten days later while I was still making plans, my hire had negotiated a deal with the client, and they changed all the locks on the offices. She and the client greeted me together and explained that my firm was no longer needed. Can you hear the china smashing? This woman had not even met the rest of the team working on the account! She looked at the invoices, knew she was making much less than the client was paying my company, and decided she could make this money herself.

She lasted 35 days with the client after that. What had now become my former client then went through three other managers within one year.

The second thief I spotted early. She asked a simple question out of turn. "How do you run credit checks?" Like the greatest spy thriller, I raised one eyebrow and answered the question in a vague dismissive fashion. Within an hour, I read her company emails to my client where they were discussing which files of mine to copy, what questions to ask me, and when was a good time for her to form her company. I greeted her at the door the next morning. I walked with her to clean out her desk, and I walked with her to the door.

When you're a big firm, you can crush problems like this. You can tie the offender up in legal battles and make them rue the day they stole from you. When you're small though, these thieves can steal your clients, supplies, money, energy and morale.

Trust your instincts. If you suspect thievery, keep your eyes open. If you have supplies, secure them and keep good inventory. If you catch one, never give a thief another chance. Your assumption because of your good nature is that they have learned their lesson. The better assumption is that they are looking to not get caught next time.

STEP 65: Trust your instincts and inventory when you suspect theft. Terminate thieves immediately.

THE TAX MAN COMETH

File some sort of tax return for your business every year. Pay the taxes. Trust me, not doing this is the one part of running a small business that will get hold of you and follow you to your grave. This, I know.

The good news is, it is much worse to file nothing than it is to make mistakes. Mistakes can be corrected, but avoidance is the nightmare you can barely wake up from. More good news is the vast amount of software tools available to help you keep your books in order.

If you have read previous chapters and are following the advice, then you are already keeping your financial records on a software system like Intuit's QuickBooks. Online software tools have reminders of all of the key dates for filing and some have e-filing built into their systems.

It is easy to get behind in these matters. Try not to. If you receive a letter from the Internal Revenue Service (IRS) open it immediately and call the person in the letter. Let them know you have received the communication and you are going to resolve the matter.

Once they know you are communicating with them, future exchanges could go more smoothly. Your tax issues will not go away until they're fully resolved, but if the process gets adversarial, they can make your life and ability to do business quite miserable.

Some states' revenue departments are even worse. They get your attention by dissolving your company first. In fourteen years, that has happened to me three times! Once, when I called, the young man said, "This is about your State taxes from seven years ago." I asked why they didn't send any written communication; he said "We did, to your address of seven years ago." Unbelievable.

If you can afford it, hire a tax attorney. We have already talked about the right attorney. Let them act as your agent to the IRS or your state. The stress of the IRS can really be unhealthy. Also, a good tax attorney can determine what is needed in short order and help resolve matters much faster. Good attorneys have the direct phone numbers to the right departments to get necessary answers. My attorney got the dissolution of my company resolved immediately. Then it was on to the next battle.

STEP 66: File taxes annually. Pay the taxes. Answer communications from the IRS immediately.

HERE COMES THE JUDGE

Unfortunately, I think it is inevitable that some municipality will summon you for something as an entrepreneur. There are so many rules of engagement and you will unwittingly break a few. Between this and some legal dispute between you and another human being, you may face a Judge or at least an Administrator. I have said many times, when cities avoid raising taxes, you better start looking at the fees. Somebody is paying more, somewhere.

Knowing that most of us microbusiness owners face this fact took the edge off for me. I have lost thousands of dollars not dealing with these matters up front. Official documents in the mail were just exhausting. I would stress out just looking at the logos on the fat envelopes with the many pieces of paper inside.

As a microbusiness, these are my suggestions for dealing with these legal challenges:

- Open the communication immediately. Even if you don't understand, focus on the court date and the dollar amount.

- Go to that courthouse at least a week before your court date. Sit there to understand the process.

- If you don't have a lawyer, look for the busiest defense lawyers there. These men/women know this landscape. Watch them and pick the ones you like. They are rarely expensive and you can quickly "interview" them on site.

- Make three copies of any defense records you have and take them with you to court. If you need the item officially entered into your record, it is best to have a copy for the court, your attorney, and yourself.

The key is, you have to deal with these items. Showing up can possibly get the fees/fines reduced and maybe get you a payment plan. Not showing up is much worse. The fines for non-appearance are as much as double the original penalty. If you continue to be non-responsive, most municipalities have the authority to tie these fines to many other services you need from your city. You may not be able to renew your business license or get permits for special events. And rest assured, if you never pay, they will get your attention when freezing the assets in your main bank account. Can you hear me now?

STEP 67: Address all legal and court challenges immediately.

MAKING TOUGH CALLS

You are going to have to make some really tough calls. Building a successful microbusiness will require you to perfect this skill. One of your relatives that you hired will have to be terminated, which could really affect your personal life. You may have to press criminal charges against someone who stole from you. You may have to let go of a really good employee because you've figured out a much more cost-efficient way to complete the task.

'

No one is going to do this for you. As the owner of the microbusiness you should not delegate these tasks. You will never know what someone else has communicated, and it is your business that's on the line for any misunderstanding.

When possible, you want to type up a quick one-pager that summarizes the facts:

- This is the relationship we had.
- This is the date it ends.
- These are the final transactions, payments, materials due, etc.
- We have no future business relationship beyond this signed agreement.

- Two signatures are required: the business owner's and the other party's.

Make two copies of this document. Both of you should sign both documents, that way both of you have original signed copies. Any final payment should be made when signing this document. It is easier to get the other party to agree to terms with money on the table. When the check clears the bank, you know this matter is closed. I prefer to present cashier's checks. I had a rich client forget to cash a regular check. She actually came to me a year later screaming: "Where's my money?" She learned that banks don't recognize vintage checks. Ugh.

STEP 68: Make tough calls yourself. Don't designate this task. When possible, create a one-page document summarizing final understandings.

BAD CREDIT

The ugly secret about starting a microbusiness is the deep dive your credit may take if you aren't starting with a huge savings. This is normal. You go from the safe and "stable" world of getting a paycheck of a set amount at a predictable time, to paying yourself a few dollars when you can. This is the microbusiness hurdle many people have a hard time getting over.

The key to making it over this hump is to redefine normal. Many corporate people try to start a microbusiness and make it look just like the job they left. This is why immigrants often do better as microbusiness owners. They don't have the same expectations of instant gratification and immediate financial success Americans tend to express.

When I started my business, I took a leap of faith (or jumped off a cliff) with an SBA loan. Prior to the business, my life could not have been more predictable. I had a corporate job and a nice paycheck. The banks saw me as a good risk. That free fall from the cliff was my first year of business. I had to spend my loan in the first six months. By the ninth month, I was out of money and mired in debt. Any money that came in went to the employees first. I only brought enough money home to put some food on the table.

None of my personal bills got paid. Once while home alone, I checked my credit score out of curiosity. In one year, my credit dropped 145 points. I screamed out loud and then sobbed uncontrollably. I sank into a deep depression until I decided to think outside of the box.

Suppose, just suppose, my self-worth wasn't tied to my credit score. What if I decided to define what success was going to mean in my life? I decided if I gained more clients, if I paid my team, if I didn't curse anyone out, and if I created meaningful ways to grow my company, then I was awesome! I decided that I had to keep a happy home for my son, and to create systems to help me keep a roof over our heads for now. I also decided not to check my credit for years. I needed to grow the business, not borrow money.

STEP 69: Understand that your credit score may drop in the beginning of a microbusiness. Don't let this hiccup deter you from moving forward.

HIDE & SEEK

When you are low on funds, when you are out of a product, or when you can't provide the service you said you would, don't hide. Be honest with the people who were counting on you. Do this as soon as possible.

So many things that are not under your control will not go as you plan. The sooner you can communicate this to the affected parties, the better the outcome for your microbusiness. Avoiding the problem guarantees the situation will be worse.

When you deliver this news, the first sentence is the apology. The second sentence is the circumstance. The third sentence is your plan to remedy the situation. The rest is extra. So you say something like, "I'm sorry to have to say this. We will not be able to pay our full balance on Saturday as planned. My goal is to have the balance to you in 10 days." This direct approach gives the recipient of bad news a chance to process the worst news first. They can then listen to the rest of your conversation. If you drag out this news or, heaven forbid, avoid this person until they have to hide or block their phone number when calling to find you, the relationship can be permanently damaged.

On the flip side, some people will hide from you. They will owe you money. Everyone is not ethical or comfortable telling others bad news upfront. You will have to hunt down these people. Ideally, this will help you understand how others feel when being avoided. This happens early in building microbusinesses. The good news is that over time, you weed out the customers and suppliers who play hide and seek. You build good trusting relationships where any unpleasant news is delivered fast and in a hurry. Those people keep you around because you are the same way.

STEP 70: Tell customers and suppliers any bad news as soon as possible with a planned remedy. Never play hide and seek with valuable relationships.

CHAPTER 11

WRONG PATH

THE $1 CAR WASH

"All we've got to do is charge less than that guy and everyone will come to us…"

I love the conversation of the new entrepreneur that starts with, "All we've got to do is …" because there is nothing "that simple." All the simple things have already been done, and all of the easy money has been made. You're going to have some serious setbacks if you think you have discovered some easy money that everyone missed.

When I started my business, I thought I would see what my competitor was charging and simply offer more service and charge less money. Who wouldn't choose my business over theirs? How could this fail? After we got everybody hooked on our product and dependent on our service, we would adjust our prices to fit our expenses and even raise our fees to make a big, fat profit.

So that's what we did. I went to great lengths to find out what our competitors were charging. And I charged less. Period. Writing this now seems so stupid, but I was committed to this strategy and it took a lot of time and effort to gather my competition's information.

The truth is that this strategy only works if you're selling illegal drugs. People have to be seriously hooked on your product to not simply make another choice. Bargain hunters will find you, but then find the next deal and drop you like a bad habit.

The time I spent should have been on my own actual costs. I had a small SBA loan, plus my own cash in the business, so the poverty path that I was on wasn't so clear. I thought aggressive efforts to get new business were simply the smartest thing to do. Soon (and I mean after a few years) I could sum up this entire strategy as the "$1 Car Wash."

You open the $1 Car Wash and have cars lined up around the block for days. You're so busy, you assume you're making money. But once you add in the water, rent, electricity and labor you are actually spending $1.56 per car! You're moving so many cars and so much cash that it takes forever to realize that you will never be profitable.

So, I didn't literally own a car wash business. The reality is that I and many people opened businesses that were very busy, but not making enough money to survive. Because I paid the rent on this day and met payroll on that day, it wasn't obvious that I was going broke. I tell you, we were posing for pictures and signing autographs! What's the problem? Everything.

Here are the facts about the $1 Car Wash model:

- People who pay the dollar still want the best service ever.
- Dollar customers tell their dollar friends and the $1 customer becomes your permanent customer. The high-end customer will never let you touch their car. Not even for $1.
- It's almost impossible to shave costs enough unless you are a mass marketer.

How did we survive this? We didn't. We had to close the proverbial $1 Car Wash, remodel, re-staff, and open the proverbial "*Deluxe, Exclusive, One-of-a-Kind Hand Car Wash*" for people who care tremendously for their cars." We created a new website, new business cards and a new logo. Keeping with the metaphor, we let the dollar clients go. Once we understood the customer we wanted, we went after the luxury cars.

STEP 71: Commit to changing course if you aren't charging enough or making a decent profit.

PIMPING AIN'T EASY

Pimps have to convince a person to do something strange for a little change. They have to convince the "john" or "mark" to pay enough money to support the pimp lifestyle. A pimp also must persuade the person he peddles to be comfortable with a tiny share of the proceeds while lavishing the rest on himself. That's a lot of hustling. That ain't easy.

If your business model includes you being off somewhere, smooth talking clients, while others do the work for you, you are headed down the wrong path. A microbusiness starts from something you can do personally. You build the business by hiring people as your business grows, but you start where you alone can begin.

If you are starting a vendor cart, then you start from what you personally can sell. If you are starting a restaurant, then you probably ought to be able to cook. If you open a bar, then you should be able to mix the drinks. You need to understand what motivates your customers and what will make your offering attractive. It's not enough to just know money can be made.

The question you should be able to answer yes to is: "If no one shows up to work today, can I still open the business and make money?" If the answer is no, then you have a big problem with your little business.

There is enough to learn while building a business. If you don't know the core business at all, then you likely are doomed. You may be the owner, but you are lacking the necessary knowledge to fix any problem. You can't even answer a specific question from a customer. Your credibility is less than zero before you get started.

Where I've seen plenty of failure is where educated people with great credit secure a loan with some collateral and blissful ignorance. They figure that they can open a hair salon and simply hire a few stylists, or they can secure a construction contract and just hire some plumbers and electricians. If a client has a bad chemical reaction in her hair or a waste stack collapses at the construction site, then the smart entrepreneur can fix this situation. The hired help has the luxury of walking off the job. That's where pimping skills are required. It takes a lot of fast talk to soothe angry customers with singed hair that you can't fix. It takes real hustle to obtain more money for additional construction repairs that you should have been aware of or don't even understand.

Entering into a business that you have little or no knowledge of isn't the recipe for a successful business. It's a juggling act for as long as you can keep it up. Let the pimps and the johns and the rest stay in the underworld. Run a business that you respect enough to learn and understand.

STEP 72: Commit to knowing how to run your core business. Do not rely on simply paying others to work for you.

THERE IS NO WIZARD

If you think a conversation with a celebrity, politician, athlete or any person of notoriety will help your business be successful you may be right. But not right away.

Many people spend an abundance of time trying to meet someone of celebrity or notoriety to either endorse their businesses or even invest. These people are asked all the time to participate in countless projects. Just as you would not invest money or time in people or projects you've never heard of, most celebrities or politicians won't either.

The reality is, an excellent product or service will attract almost everyone. A great new food business or a great new day spa will practically promote itself. Once you have stabilized your business, you can seek support. It won't be random and wide-eyed hope; it will be laser-focused because you know your product and your customer and who can actually carry the right message forward.

When you are trying to figure out what your stumbling blocks are in the business, your answer should not be: "If only I could meet _____, we could be successful."

There is no wizard. There is only a better product or a better service at a better convenience at a better price. The solutions to those four items will draw customers. Once you have mastered this, the fame and fortune may come.

STEP 73: Change your strategy if you find yourself trying to meet celebrities, politicians or athletes in order to improve your business.

ALL STYLE NO SUBSTANCE

Do not spend a great deal of time being seen on the scene. Networking has its purpose. If you don't know exactly why you are attending an event, don't go.

My first few years of business, I wanted to get out there and let people know we are here! My business is alive. I am the one to do business with. I read the society pages, so I knew the events I wanted to attend. My goal was to attend at least two big events a month. With the ticket costs averaging $150 per person, I spent at least $4,000 per year on these events, not including the ancillary costs of parking, gas and new clothes. Did I get any work from being seen on the scene? No. Am I saying you should never attend these events? No.

There's a skill to attending the appropriate events. You develop it over time. You have specific plans and specific people you want to meet. You develop specific questions and look for specific follow-up call times or meeting dates.

Before you invest in any networking event, ask yourself:
- Do I have a meaningful pitch to give right now?
- What three people do I know are likely to be there?
- What would I like to say to those people?

Attend the event, connect with the three people and then leave. Hanging around is not the highest and best use of your time. Remaining too long and drinking too much can rarely help but easily hurt. Plus, you are busy.

I knew a guy I called Dapper Dan. This man has a business that involves mechanical engineers, electrical contractors and the like. His logo was awesome; his office was spaciously located in the heart of the city. He had two secretaries, some administrators, an accountant, a media specialist and a lawyer on retainer. Dapper Dan was one of the best-dressed men I've ever met. His conference rooms and reception areas were filled with pictures of him with very important people. In them, Dapper Dan is smiling with everyone from local politicians to movie stars to presidents to let everyone know how important he is to the creation of wealth and success in his business. Every time there was a new opening, an important gala or a significant charity gala, Dapper Dan was there!

At first, I was very impressed with his position. Isn't that one of the many ways you measure success? The truth is, we used to value success by all of these trophies and this enormous staff. It screamed to people, we are busy. We are successful. Many people, including Dapper Dan, think that if you focus on the appearance of success, then you can *fake it until you make it.*

This isn't the 1980s. What matters now are success stories. You need photos with people for whom you have made money, saved money or provided a valuable service.

STEP 74: Determine if there is real value in attending a networking event. Identify whom you will connect with and what you plan to say.

NO MONEY, NO GLORY

You have to make sure that you are making money. Very little else matters if there is no profit.

During year four of my business, I hired a CFO. Not because I felt I needed him. I was struggling a little with wide-eyed enthusiasm compensating for my lack of profits. I really wanted him to tell me how great I was, growing my little business from nothing. He took a brief look at my books and said, "You're going to fail if you keep this up."

I was livid at his quick assessment. I had staff moving about, plenty of clients, a desk full of work, and still had plenty of things to do! What he said is not what I expected to hear. This kind of cynicism kills a business. My ego and I double-teamed him. We let him have it. When I was done yelling, I was tired. He said, "Are you finished?" I wasn't done, but I was winded. He then calmly explained to me, using a pen and a plain sheet of paper, how expenses were far exceeding our income. Obvious, right? Not so much!

As a property management firm, we were adding clients with buildings to manage left and right, and I wasn't adding staff or office space, so my mental math said we were growing. Wrong. The gas alone needed to service these tiny new spread-out clients was killing us. The expense of taking on new clients, integrating them into the software, talking to new clients with all new questions, and adding the clients to the maintenance route was killing us softly.

My new CFO told me the size of the smallest client I could take without losing my shirt. Less than 5% of our clients fit that model. My SBA loan kept me from seeing this slow drip of imminent demise since my bank account was still in the black.

I cried that night, because I was moving full steam ahead on the wrong road. The CFO was kind enough to simply identify the cliff we were headed toward. But each of these clients represented a relationship. How was I going to break up with all of these people? Who could possibly love my company after this? This was as good a place as any to start phasing out the company. I still had the shirt on my back. I could sever this team so as to not to ruin their lives completely.

Then I thought about Listerine. Two men formulated it as a surgical antiseptic in 1879. It was later sold in distilled form as both a floor cleaner and a cure for gonorrhea. It wasn't until 1920 that the company started marketing the product for bad breath.[1] In seven years, their sales went from $115,000 to $8 million. There is life after the initial miscalculation.

STEP 75: Make sure that you have made more money than you have spent every day. If not, correct that immediately.

---

[1] http://www.listerine.co.za/history/history-brand

NO UPFRONT FEES

Businesses with upfront fees have long fascinated me. They convince you that *if you are serious, then you must pay for their services first*--as they are the experts! Once you put your money on the table, you should brace yourself for the explanation as to why they will NOT be able to do more for you. They will also tell you how you brought this failure onto yourself.

These people show up when you are at your darkest point. That's because you can't even see or hear such nonsense when your company is sailing along. Much like those crazy emails that tell you of the rich uncle who left you millions in foreign dollars, you would have deleted this noise in less than 10 seconds if you weren't desperate. You need money, the bank has rejected you. Your friends and family avert their eyes when they see you coming. You've got to make payroll, and the phone will be disconnected soon. You're glad to see the red light on the power strip is still on when you come into the office. This means the lights are still on. This is usually when you're introduced to the finance guy (or gal).

Here's the pitch: This consultant will speak immediately of some transaction that was huge! The implication is their involvement helped bring that money across the finish line. It's never really clear if they can get you debt financing or equity. Your devastating credit or dire situation isn't insurmountable, but will cost you extra. You toss logic out the window. "This must be how it's done. This must be how people stay afloat. If I borrow just a little more money to pay this consultant, then I can quickly pay it back along with everyone else I owe in the universe and get back on top!"

Rest assured. You'll just owe one more person. That money is not coming.

I can still remember sitting in my office in Chicago talking to a finance guy in St. Louis. I had met this guy from one of those entrepreneurial organizations. He was describing his business model to the group and I said to myself: "This middleman-model has no future." He was the guy who was supposed to help you find the right bank. Why would I need help finding a bank in a major city? If I tripped and fell, I'd find three banks before I hit the ground.

But now I'm broke. He's explaining to me, for a $2,500 consulting fee and completing this form, he can get me the $250,000 I should have gotten from my initial bank loan.

My better self started yelling at the broke me, "Come ON! You know better than this!" But my receptionist steps in to hand me a message. Another bill collector just called.

Allocating this $2,500 is a real commitment, but I'm going to do it. I've squelched the voice of the logical me. I'm just going to phone a friend to get some moral support.

"Ang, I've never seen anyone get money from the man with the up-front fee," he says.

In that one sentence, he averted my business from failure. And this was a new friend. He echoed what I already knew. Money doesn't change hands that way. Wherever you get financing, that source will connect with you directly. Whether it's a bank, a personal loan, or some sort of fund, you will connect directly. An appropriate middleman may have a success fee. He/she gets paid at the closing table. My new friend said, "I wish I had the courage to just ask someone that back when I ran out of money!" Yeah, well women stop and ask, I thought.

STEP 76: Commit to never seeking financial support from someone requiring an up-front fee. Commit to only paying success fees.

THE POSERS

Remember that entrepreneurship is lonely. You make your plans and the natural instinct is to seek approval from someone. There's nothing wrong with making sure your decisions are vetted with another party. If you don't have the experience to know who to trust with insecurities or who to take advice from, you will spend time with the wrong person who looks right. Enter the poser.

These are the friends or family that have some expertise in various professions. They love your entrepreneurial spirit but will never take the risk of actually starting a business. But they will take an equity piece of your business or your large contract to help you out. They have been at the table of really big deals and you haven't. So there is an illusion of missing information, this person probably knows something you don't. If you don't add them to the team, your team will not be as strong. Resist the urge to add people to your team who enter the picture this way.

You know your business. You know your customer and your client. Just like the opening sequence of the original TV show, "Mission Impossible," you decide who should be on your team to best execute your strategy.

Be leery of someone who says: "I'll take 15% of the deal to help you out" or "I'll take the cash from the door because I'm the promoter." Instead, you should decide in the beginning what is the right team for your business. You instead would say to your colleague, "I would like you to join this team for $_____. The deliverable will be X" or "I will pay you $500 if the crowd tonight exceeds 250 people."

I once had a dapper young man insist that he get 25% of any work I got from an introduction he was willing to make for me. In my first year of business, I would have considered it. I had seen that kind of thing in the movies. But he offered that in year 12. It took everything I had to politely finish the conversation. As a diehard optimist, I saw the conversation as a compliment. He thought my projects were valuable enough to steal.

Usually the posers come to you with the offer. You may have been seeking advice in general or just having a conversation. These offers initially feel like a relief. Somebody wants to walk this path with you. This is rarely a good deal.

STEP 77: Avoid adding the posers to your team. Make sure you have brought everyone to the table because it makes sense for your microbusiness.

CHAPTER 12

IN THE END

REMEMBER TO HAVE FUN

I love having a microbusiness. I would not live my life any other way. I have had jobs. I understand the security of a regular paycheck, but it does not come close to the freedom I have of living this life on my own terms.

When you have chosen a business that you are excited about, you can really have fun. Make sure you schedule fun with your family and friends. Make sure you schedule fun with your work team.

Consider signing your company's team up for local walk-a-thons or volunteering at community picnics and parades. Having the team wear company t-shirts helps promote camaraderie as well as promotes your business to the locals.

When I get too deep into the weeds of the business with the bills, the problems or the uncertainty, I take a walk. Fortunately, Chicago has beautiful lakefronts and neighborhoods. I simply stroll to remind myself that I can. Ownership allows me this freedom. I visualize a less stressful scenario for my business and me. I count my blessings. I may phone a friend.

I have a coffee mug I purchased when I started my business. It says: "I'm the boss, I can do whatever I want." I don't have it in the office. I don't want to appear like an overlord. But when I'm home and feeling off, it's the first cup I reach for when making coffee. It makes me smile.

STEP 78: Schedule fun activities for you and your team that promote camaraderie and the business. Schedule fun for yourself to avoid burnout.

GROWING... PAINS?

Let's say you have hit the spot! You have a product your customer base loves. Your business is running like a well-oiled machine. There are always set backs, but you can handle them as fast as they come. You have a good first lieutenant and you are able to take vacations and breaks while your microbusiness still functions.

Do you expand your business or maintain what you have? These are nice problems to have. And there are plenty of books, consultants and workshops to give you advice on this type of growth. There are recommendations regarding the proximity of your locations, one to another. There are decisions as to whether or not to take your production off-shore. There are decisions about whether to take on huge debt or a substantial equity partner.

You're going from a microbusiness to a "small business." There is an entire ecosystem around this type of business. Businesses with investors and over 20 employees have more moving parts. They have a lot more variables to consider. Many of the concerns were not covered in this book.

My advice would be to continue to function with a microbusiness mentality. All of the fancy financing and strategy consultants won't know your business the way you do. But if your goal is to franchise your food business or sell your product to a big box retailer, then you need to bring in the expert consultants.

That is a whole different ball game.

STAY, GROW OR GO?

The entrepreneurial spirit is all about choices. You have success with your business and you are at a crossroads. Do you want to continue doing this? Don't be afraid to walk away. Do something else! Just as in leaving a job, there is a smart way to exit a microbusiness.

As microbusiness owners we care about the community. No one wants to see a vacant retail space in his or her community. If you have a storefront, consider turning over the business to a family member or employee. They can buy you out with a flat fee or they can buy you out with a longer-term loan you make to them allowing them to pay you from business operations. The business itself can be the collateral. You will know who you think is capable enough to run the operation.

If you don't sell to anyone, then let the landlord know as soon as possible that you will not be renewing the lease. Plan your exit and notify your customers of the closing date. This will accelerate sales and give people a chance to say farewell.

No matter what industry you are in, put this information on your website and social media. Contact your accountant and attorneys to file the appropriate paperwork to close and or dissolve the operation formally. You don't want fees or debts to mount based on your failure to end the business properly.

I have started quite a few businesses. I used to joke: I've started more microbusinesses than most men have shoes. Some were solo efforts and some were collaborations. The key thing is that I moved forward on ideas that I thought were good. I pursued my passions. I did not measure success on the false sense of security of having a job. I measured success on the fact that I was free enough to believe that the next idea was the best idea and if it didn't sell I was smart enough to keep going.

Whatever you decide, first acknowledge the freedom and success of being able to make that decision.

THERE'S ALWAYS TOMORROW

Every day--amid all the crazy situations, the computer crashes, the overbearing clients, the bonanzas and complete busts--I live for this. I'm a serial entrepreneur.

I can't imagine life any other way. I'm like you! We know who we are.

We are the ones who figure we are the perfect people to solve certain problems. Working for anyone else only detracts from our most efficient solution. One of my colleagues said it best, "I work for myself because no one else will do things my way!"

All of the chapters in this book are lessons I've learned. And most of them I learned in the School of Hard Knocks. I now know storms come and go. Only now, I can feel them coming like any other animal in the jungle that runs to higher ground when the earth tremors.

I no longer fear failure. I face it quickly and think, "How can we remedy this?" I know the solution is buried in the problem, so I dig deep.

The goal of this book is to help you understand that you have the power to create your microbusiness now. It's also to help you see some of the potential hurdles coming. There's nothing wrong with being prepared for a storm.

I didn't go to an Ivy League school. I'm from middle-class parents in a middle-class community in America. I've never made a multimillion-dollar deal. But I've employed some good people from my community. I've put my son through college and later sent him to live and work abroad, bought a house and a building, traveled a lot, and left some places better than I found them. I don't have an alarm clock, but I'm wildly excited about each new day.

I built cool microbusinesses that I'm proud of. I hope you will, too.

ACKNOWLEDGEMENTS

Deciding to write a book to share my experiences was a long journey. I made so many mistakes in entrepreneurship that I felt more like the village idiot than someone who had amassed true wisdom about microbusinesses. It was my lifelong friends/brothers from college, Reggie Summerrise and Shawn Brown that started their businesses before me that kept encouraging me and smiling as I sat in the corner terrified to start the next day. I owe them a lot.

Once I got the courage to write it, Denise Gritsch and Melissa Traywick were the true coaches that made me believe I had valuable information to share. They stuck with me as I was plagued with doubt. Jean Williams was a true gem to review the book and share sage advice. Lyneir Richardson is a very close friend from whom I learned many lessons. He is a seasoned and successful entrepreneur and one of the first people I met as an entrepreneur that I was honest with about my business. To this day, he is my closest collaborator on "Now Money". I still use my own steps!

My mentors have to be mentioned as well. Nancy Pacher and Steve Wolf were essential to my success as a businesswoman. They gave me the information straight with no chaser. When I was off course, they told me. You cannot succeed without people like that in your life.

There are countless friends and colleagues who encouraged me to move forward with this book. But my son, Steven Ballard and two of my best friends Robert Dabney, the book's Editor and my Sorority Sister, Constance Gully were the ones that rode the roller coaster of emotions and words and phrases and clauses during the months of writing. I am more appreciative of them than they will ever know.

I would be remiss if I didn't mention my Mother, Ruby Ford, my Grandmother, Edna Murray and my Aunt Jackie Crawford. Between the three of them were five Master's Degrees and one all-but-dissertation (my Mom's). They held careers as educators in Chicago's Public School system until retirement. It was not easy for them to watch me flail around with these small business endeavors. But they supported me. My Aunt bought my first business cards. My grandmother bought all of my paper supplies until her death. My Mom loaned me her car after I totaled mine! She thought this book was a great idea. They've all transitioned from this life, but the best of them still lives in me. Combined they taught thousands of students. I hope some people learn from this book. Then I will have carried on their legacies as an Educator.

Grandma, Aunt Jackie & Mom

INDEX

Made in the USA
Middletown, DE
22 June 2016